DUCK AND SWAN

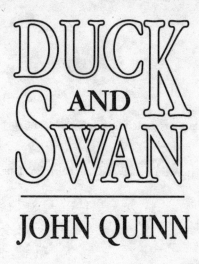

DUCK AND SWAN

JOHN QUINN

POOLBEG

•

The publishers gratefully acknowledge the support of

The Arts Council/An Chomhairle Ealaíon.

•

First published 1993 by
Poolbeg,
A division of Poolbeg Enterprises Ltd,
Knocksedan House,
123 Baldoyle Industrial Estate, Dublin 13.
Reprinted December 1993

© John Quinn 1993

The moral right of the author has been asserted.

A catalogue record for this book is available from the British Library.

ISBN 1 85371 317 1

Cover illustration by Judith O'Dwyer
Cover design by Poolbeg Group Services Ltd
Set by Mac Book Limited
Printed by The Guernsey Press Company Limited,
Vale, Guernsey, Channel Islands.

*For the children who asked for more
and for the children who asked questions.
Don't ever stop asking questions!*

A NOTE ON THE AUTHOR

John Quinn was born in Co. Meath and worked as a teacher before becoming a radio producer in the Education Department of RTE. *The Summer of Lily and Esme* was his first work of fiction and second children's book, and the winner of the 1992 Irish Children's Book Trust Bisto Book of the Year award.

PRAISE FOR *THE SUMMER OF LILY AND ESME*

"The tone is lyrical and reflective, the narrative compelling and the setting—present and past— evoked with an excellent sense of contemporary detail."

Robert Dunbar, *The Irish Times*

"A piece of writing breathtaking for its simplicity and sheer readability...highly recommended."

Books Ireland

"If there is such a thing as an instant classic, then this is one."

Books Ireland

Contents

Chapter 1

Emer

"Miss! Miss!" The girls clamoured excitedly around their teacher as she emerged from her car.

"Miss! Laura Daly's not coming!"

"Miss! She broke her arm and—"

"All right girls. I know! I know! I know all about Laura falling off her bike and breaking her arm. And having suspected head injuries. She was a naughty girl not to wear her helmet, wasn't she?" The girls drew back from their teacher. Trust Miss Dunne to turn Laura's accident into a safety lesson. "Anyway, I've just come from her home and her parents tell me she's quite comfortable in hospital. We'll have to send her a big get well card, won't we girls?"

"Yes, Miss Dunne."

Emer Healy wandered away from the fringe of the crowd of girls. She felt an emptiness in the bottom of her stomach. She hadn't wanted to go on this school tour from the start. She was worried about her mother's illness which had dragged on since Christmas. It was now May and, despite several visits to the hospital, her mother remained weak and listless. Emer had offered to stay at home today to look after her mother, but she had insisted that Emer should go. The school arranged separate day trips for the boys and girls and today

Miss Dunne was taking the girls to Dublin.

"It's a day out in Dublin and you'll see lots of interesting things at the museum and the Zoo. I'll manage. Marion has a half-day, so that will be a help." Marion's response to her mother had been predictable. At fifteen years of age, three years older than her sister, Marion Healy reckoned she had a lot of living to do and looking after her sick mother was not her ideal way of spending a half-day off school.

"Does anyone realise that I have a Junior Cert exam in three weeks time?" Marion sighed. "And that I need to do lots of revision? I am under a lot of stress. Does anyone realise that?"

Emer smiled. She knew her sister's "revision" would include strolling around the streets of Galway with her pals, chatting up the boys and smoking the odd cigarette.

"You can revise at home, dear," her mother replied softly. "You'll have no interruptions—Johnny's going to a birthday party." Johnny was the tail-end of the family. He was four—a very lively four-year-old.

"Typical," Marion sniffed. "Johnny's off to a birthday party; Mademoiselle here is off to Dublin for the day, while I—whose career is in the balance—must stay at home. Typical!"

"It's only a half-day, Marion, and it's Emer's educational tour," her mother argued weakly.

"Little Miss Swot!" Marion hissed to her sister. Emer pulled a face in return but the arguments ended with the arrival of their father, driving a council lorry. Marion knew that she did not dare put on her performance before her father. "All right," she snapped quickly as she watched her father leap from the cab. "I'll be here. But remember if I fail French in the Junior Cert...."

2

And now Emer's best pal, Laura Daly, had gone and fallen off the bike and couldn't come on the tour. Emer thought of hiding in the bicycle shed and letting them go without her but at that moment the bus lumbered into view and shuddered to a halt in the lay-by outside the school. The girls shrieked excitedly and rushed towards the bus.

"Now girls, please!" Miss Dunne screamed above the din. "In twos, girls. In twos. You know the drill!" The girls grabbed their partners and held hands while chattering non-stop. Emer sighed. Laura Daly was her partner, so she just drifted along in the queue to board the bus, clutching her rucksack with both hands. As she passed the rear of the bus, the driver suddenly revved the engine and the bus shuddered as it belched poisonous black fumes from its exhaust. Three-to-four hours in that thing, Emer thought. I wish I had let Marion do her "revision".

"Now girls. Remember!" Miss Dunne tightly gripped a seat on either side of her, as the bus swayed and bumped its way down the narrow country road. "You're representing Tubberfinn today, so I want everyone on their best behaviour! I—" There was a loud burp to her left. Josie Byrne's round fat face blushed as she stuffed the last few crisps from a packet into her mouth. The girls giggled loudly.

"Really, Josephine Byrne! Do you have to start eating so soon?"

"I'm sorry, Miss," Josie mumbled.

"And we never talk with our mouths full! I want Tubberfinn to be proud of us. Manners, courtesy, resp—" There was a mighty crack as the seat in front of Emer collapsed, causing its occupant, Sharon Duffy, to shriek in horror. Uproar followed as the bus was stopped and the driver inspected the damaged seat. Several other girls bounced up and down on their seats to test them.

"Please Miss. All I did was lean back!" Sharon sobbed.

"All right! All right! There's no need for tears, Sharon. Let you and Julie sit up at the front beside me!"

Order was restored and the tour got under way again. Emer stretched her legs under the broken seat and looked at the large red letters that were peeling away from the windows—TOBIN LUXURY TRAVEL. She smiled and closed her eyes.

Three noisy, hot and fume-filled hours later they tumbled gratefully out of the bus into the bright sunlight of a Dublin street. Miss Dunne lined them up on the pavement and gave them a final pep-talk. "Now girls, remember, we're Tubberfinn girls and we're on our best behaviour. Manners, courtesy, respect—"

A refuse-lorry rumbled by, drowning out her words. Three workers hung carelessly on to a bar over the platform on the rear. One of them, a barrel-chested balding man with a cigarette tucked behind his ear, waved to the girls and bellowed across the street: "Hey, teacher! Give us a kiss!"

It was Miss Dunne's turn to blush. The girls sniggered behind their hands but the teacher quickly composed herself. "As I was saying girls—manners, courtesy, respect—and dignity!" She distributed worksheets among the class. "I want each one of you to fill in your worksheet as you go around the museum. Simply observe, girls! Observe!" They trooped into the museum.

"Simply observe, girls!" Josie Byrne mimicked as she waddled through the museum gate, last in the Tubberfinn line.

The museum was very interesting. They wandered from room to room marvelling at the relics of past centuries and often giggling at the dress of times past. They compared notes on their worksheet entries. Someone called out a question. "Why did the Viking have a bowl buried with him?"

"Guess what I have written," Jenny Gavin boasted. "So that no one could steal his corn flakes!" The laughter echoed round the great museum hall until Miss Dunne called the girls to order. "Girls! Girls!" she whispered aloud. "Manners! Courtesy! Respect!"

As they worked their way around the museum, Emer thought of her mother and how she was feeling. She hoped that Marion was not moaning about her "revision".

The bus was just about to pull away when it was noticed that Josie Byrne was missing. "Don't panic, girls," Miss Dunne said calmly, "We'll find her!"

"Here she is, Miss!"

The stout figure of Josie came puffing up the street, waving her anorak in one hand and her worksheet in the other.

"Really, Josephine!" Miss Dunne admonished her. "Where have on earth have you been?"

"I was in the loo, Miss, and—"

"Well you should have informed me—and you were in the *toilet*, Josephine."

"Yes, Miss," Josie gasped. "I would have been out in time but the door of the loo was stuck!"

They sang their way across the city, cheering and waving at whoever would take notice of them. They reached the Phoenix Park. The bus was parked outside the park gates and Miss Dunne led the Tubberfinn line into the vast expanse of the Park where the girls ran free and enjoyed a picnic lunch.

Miss Dunne was determined that the tour would be educational. When they entered the Zoo gates, she gathered the class around her and gave a talk on some of the animals they were likely to see. She then distributed more worksheets.

"Ah, Miss," the class chorused. "Not again!"

"Yes again, girls. Your parents didn't part with their hard-earned money just for you to idle the day away! You came here to learn. So go and learn. We assemble here at five o'clock. And remember, girls—" Josie Byrne got the words out before the teacher. "Manners, respect—and dignity," she muttered viciously.

"Are you all right, Josephine?" Miss Dunne enquired in a cold voice.

"Yes, Miss. Just a bit hungry, Miss."

"Really Josephine. You must control your eating habits. All right, girls!" She clapped her hands briskly. "To work!"

Although the class had the freedom of the Zoo for two hours, the girls were divided into groups according to the worksheets they had been given. Emer was assigned to the reptile house with Jenny Gavin and Paula Power. They answered questions about anacondas and alligators, pythons and lizards. Jenny could never resist playing a trick on anyone and when Josie Byrne left her worksheet down on a bench to buy a candy-floss, it was too good an opportunity to miss. To the question, "What is the natural habitat of the baboon?" Jenny wrote "Tubberfinn."

The afternoon passed all too quickly and at five o'clock Miss Dunne was pacing up and down waiting for the Tubberfinn line to be completed. Inevitably Josie Byrne was last to arrive, dreamily eating a banana.

"Josephine, do you ever stop eating, child?"

"Please, Miss, I bought it for the monkeys but the keeper said I wasn't to feed him, so—"

"Oh come on, child. In your line. In twos, girls. In twos."

It was a relief to sink into the seat on Tobin's bus. It was only then that Emer realised how tired she was. She was glad now that no one was sitting beside her. She could relax, maybe sleep. There was an excited chatter among the girls as they relived the events of the day, but by the time the bus had wound its way out of the city on the road west, a general quietness had descended on the girls. That quiet was suddenly shattered by a loud shriek from Miss Dunne.

"Josephine Byrne, report to me first thing on Monday morning about your Zoo worksheet!"

Emer didn't dare look at Jenny Gavin but she heard the stifled laughter that came from Jenny's seat. Josie shrugged her shoulders and opened a bag of crisps.

The bus chased the lowering sun across the flat midlands. Emer closed her eyes and slid down into her seat, stretching her legs beneath the seat that had collapsed under Sharon Duffy. There was a dark bundle under the seat. Sharon's anorak probably she thought. Emer poked at it so that she could stretch out fully. To her surprise the bundle spun around to face her. Emer felt the back of her neck go rigid. Her throat went dry. She felt the colour drain from her face. The bundle unfolded slowly, noiselessly. Emer found herself staring at the face of a boy, a black boy, whose bright piercing eyes half-pleaded, half-commanded her not to do or say anything.

Chapter 2

Duck

E mer rounded her lips to ask a question. It could have been where, who, what? But none of those would come. Her face froze as she fixed her eyes on the boy, whose only gesture was to place a finger on his own lips, requesting silence. Emer slowly drew her legs out from under the collapsed seat and sat upright, never taking her eyes off the intruder. If anyone had cared to look Emer's way at that moment, they would have sensed that something was seriously wrong, but the class had divided into little clusters that sang and laughed or played games and paid no attention to the solitary girl near the rear of the bus.

Emer's mind began to unlock. Who was this boy? Why was he here? What did he hope to achieve by hiding on the bus? As if reading her mind, the boy pointed to his watch and closed his eyes, miming sleep. She found herself obeying his command but, with her eyes closed, her mind raced even faster. Where was the boy going? How would he get off the bus without being seen? She would have to speak to him. Inevitably, Josie Byrne gave her the opportunity.

"Please, Miss Dunne, can we stop at the next town? I'm dying to go to the loo—toilet!" she corrected herself. Miss Dunne sighed and looked to the driver. They had little option but to stop when a chorus of "Me too's" supported Josie's request. Emer feigned sleep and slid her rucksack across the floor in front of her, just in case anyone looked too closely. She opened her eyes very slowly and waited for a few moments to make sure everyone had gone.

"Is it all clear? Can I come out and stretch myself?"

"No! No! Some of the girls are just outside the shop. Stretch yourself out but stay on the floor."

He did as she asked. Emer was amazed at how he had managed to fold his body into such a confined space. He didn't seem to be as tall as she was but it was quite a feat.

"Now would you mind telling me what you're doing on our bus?" As she asked the question, Emer knew she sounded like Miss Dunne.

"Having me dinner! What does it look like I'm doing?" His attitude annoyed her.

"Look if you want to be smart, the driver is just outside—"

"All right. Keep your shirt on! I just thought it was obvious that I'm on the hop."

"On the hop?"

"Yeh! On the run. You see I killed me granny, blew up the school, stole me da's car—"

"Very funny! Look, you've only got five minutes until they all come back here so—"

"OK. Here's the story. Me da was from Africa. You noticed? He went back there. Me ma shacked up with this geezer who hates my guts. I left home. Went on the streets. Got into trouble. Put into care. Got fed up with all that and decided to get out of Dublin. Saw this busload of rednecks going into the Zoo. Hopped aboard when the driver wasn't looking and here I am!"

9

Emer bristled at the word "rednecks" but decided this was not the time to raise the question of colour.

"Have you anything to eat? I'm starving!"

"I have an apple...."

"It'll do!" He reached out a hand before Emer had even begun to look for the apple.

"Why don't you make a run for it now when there's no one about?" she asked, handing him the apple.

"Where are we?"

"Kinnegad, I think."

"Where's that?"

"About forty miles from Dublin."

"Not far enough. Where are youse going?"

"To County Galway. We're from Tubberfinn. There's not much there—for someone like you, I mean. Just farms—sheep and cattle and things."

"Real redneck country! Just what I want," he mumbled through the last mouthful of apple.

That's twice, Emer thought. If he mentions redneck again....

"That's the first thing I've had since breakfast. And breakfast was two bananas I nicked off a stall."

"You stole them?"

"What did you want me to do? Write a cheque?"

Emer smiled and reached into her anorak pocket. She fished out the money she had left. Seventy-two pence. She shoved the anorak towards him.

"Wrap yourself in that and fold yourself up again. They'll be back in a minute." She dashed out of the bus and up the street towards a neon take-away sign, arriving back just as the last stragglers were boarding the bus. She bent down in her seat as if to tie her lace and shoved the warm package under the anorak. "Here—chips!" she whispered.

The bus moved off again and soon the noise levels rose as the chatter and laughter echoed around the bus. Suddenly above the din the shrill voice of Miss Dunne called out, "Chips! I smell chips! Who's eating chips?" Emer sucked her breath in sharply. She had not reckoned on the smell of the chips being detected. There was a moment's lull in the chatter.

"Me. Sorry, Miss. Would you like one?"

Emer breathed a long sigh of relief. Good old Josie!

"Josephine Byrne, really. I will have to talk to your mother about your eating habits!"

Emer lay back in her seat and poked the anorak playfully with her toe. A dusky finger slid out and wagged at her. She smiled and closed her eyes in thought. What had she got herself into? Why did she cover up for this boy? Cover up. With her anorak! That's funny. Who was he, though? Maybe he had committed a serious crime. Maybe he had stolen more than two bananas. Maybe she should tell Miss Dunne. Now. The driver could then drive up to the garda station in the next town. Maybe there was a reward. Maybe....

Emer awoke with a jolt as the bus vaulted a hump-back bridge. The girls shrieked as coats and bags tumbled out of the luggage-rack overhead. Brennan's Bridge! They were nearly home. She poked at the bundle under the collapsed seat. She presumed he was still there. The close-cropped head appeared cautiously from beneath the anorak. "What was that?" he muttered. "Nearly split me bleedin' head off the seat!"

Emer glared at him and bent down to search in her rucksack. "Whisht! They'll hear you! It was a bridge. We're nearly home. What are you going to do?"

11

"Make a run for it! I'm good at that."

"No. That wouldn't work. Put the anorak on and cover up your head with the hood. Then wait till I tell you when to run."

"I can look after myself—"

"Shush!" She shoved the rucksack right in front of his face.

"Well, Emer. I didn't realise you were down here on your own all the time or I would have joined you earlier!" Miss Dunne eased herself into the seat beside Emer. Emer gasped in horror as the teacher's sandal brushed against what was obviously the boy's knee. "You look a bit pale, child. Are you all right?"

"I'm fine, Miss. I was asleep for most of the journey. I—I just woke up!"

"Well, you're the lucky one. With the noise and the smell of Josephine Byrne's chips there was no chance of me sleeping. I can still smell those chips—even down here!" Emer swallowed hard. She was looking anxiously out the window, hoping the school would soon come into view. A sudden squall sent huge raindrops careering across the window. "Is anybody meeting you, Emer?"

"No. I have my bike. I'll be all right."

"Nonsense. You'll be drenched. I'll give you a lift. Leave your bike in the school."

"But—"

Miss Dunne was already returning to her seat at the front of the bus. Emer bit her lip in frustration. What would she do now? The bus slowed down as it reached the school. She bent down to get her rucksack and poked at the bundle under the seat. "When I tell you—run!" she whispered. There was a mumbled reply from beneath the anorak.

12

The rain scudded even more intensely as the bus pulled into the school lay-by. A line of cars was parked along the school wall. The girls emerged excitedly, sheltering under anoraks, plastic bags, rucksacks—anything that would protect them from the driving rain. Although it was only ten o'clock, the summer evening had grown murky under leaden clouds. Figures called out from under umbrellas.

"Jenny—over here! Bring Paula with you."

"Sharon—quickly!"

Emer waited until last to leave the bus. She surveyed the frantic scene from the door of the bus.

"Bye! See you Monday!"

"Call over on Sunday!"

"Can't. We're going to Galway. Bye!"

Someone up there is looking after the runaway, Emer thought.

"Oh—forgot my anorak!" she announced loudly and dashed back into the bus. "Now!" she whispered. "Quickly." The boy slithered backwards from under the seat, stood up and stretched himself fully with relief. He carried a small hold-all which Emer had not noticed until now. "Don't just stand there!" Emer hissed. "Go! To the bicycle shed over there!" she pointed. "And keep the hood of that anorak up!" The boy flashed his wide eyes at her and skipped along the passageway. He was almost upended by a plump figure reversing on hands and knees from between two seats. It had to be Josie Byrne. No one else was that size, even on hands and knees. Emer literally shoved the boy out the door before asking "What's wrong, Josie?"

"My jumbo stick of rock," Josie mumbled. "Souvenir of Kinnegad. Bought it for my kid brother and can't find

13

it now."

"I'm sure it will turn up, Josie. The driver will—"

"It was that Jenny Gavin. I know it! Too smart for her boots."

Emer left Josie to continue the search and jumped from the bus, right into the path of Miss Dunne.

"There you are, child. I've been looking everywhere for you!"

"I—I was helping Josie look for her stick of rock."

"Josie!" Miss Dunne sighed the name wearily. "Now come on into the car or you'll be drenched."

"I—I just have to check that my bike is OK. Won't be a minute!" She was scurrying through the puddles before the teacher could reply. She ran through the gloom of the bicycle shed. Hers was the only bicycle there but there was no sign of the boy. Had he been caught or had he kept running?

"Up here!" The voice startled her from the dark overhead. He was perched on a crossbeam.

"God, you frightened the daylights out of me! How did you get up there?"

"You learn things," he said simply.

"Will you be all right here for the night?"

"'Course!"

"You can hold on to my anorak—till tomorrow. I'll bring you some food in the morning."

"Don't bother. I'll move on."

"Where? You don't know where you are—you'd be spotted before you went a mile."

"Well just bring me a tin of white paint then—"

"Very funny!"

Emer heard Miss Dunne's voice calling her name.

"Old Frosty-face is looking for you!"

14

"I must go. And you'd better stay!"

"OK. I'll have sausages and toast—not before ten o'clock!" He affected a grand accent.

"Fat chance! Goodbye!" She paused.

"What's your name anyway?"

"Me mates call me 'Duck'."

"Duck?" She stifled a giggle.

"Yeh. Quack! What's yours?"

"Emer!"

"Emer?" He snorted.

"What's wrong with it?" she snapped.

"Nothin'! It's a real redneck name, isn't it?"

Emer bit her lip sharply and ran out into the ever-blackening night.

Chapter 3

The Chapel

The rain cleared during the night and Emer was awakened by the strong early morning sunlight filtering into the bedroom. To be more correct, she was roused by her brother Johnny, who was awakened by the strong sunlight which filtered into the room they shared. Emer was tired and kept her eyes shut while Johnny conversed with the plastic giraffe she had bought him in Dublin. When he had tired of the giraffe, he turned to his sister.

"Emer!"

"Mmm!"

"What's a Zoo?"

"Place where they keep lots of animals and birds."

"Is there a jaff?"

"Mmm. Just like yours, but he's as tall as a tree."

"Is there a monkey?"

"Lots of them. There was one just like you."

"Was his name Johnny?"

"Don't know. Probably."

"Is there a tiger?"

"Yes." Emer was wearying of the child's endless questions.

"Will the tiger eat the jaff?"

"No. They're in different houses." Emer slid out of

bed. She was totally awake now. She looked across the bright morning fields towards Tubberfinn National School. She could just see the roof of the school in the distance. She wondered how Duck was, if he had slept in the bicycle shed or if he had moved on as he had threatened. "Come on, Johnny. Time for breakfast!"

She cooked an extra four sausages and a rasher for Duck. She hoped no one would notice. Certainly she couldn't go on doing this. She would have to talk to Duck about his plans.

Her father joined them in the kitchen. "There's no lying on on a Saturday morning with a pair of chatterboxes like you around. A pair of jackdaws!" He ruffled Johnny's hair.

"'Twas all his fault," Emer explained.

"Want to go to the Zoo," Johnny cried.

"When you're bigger, little man," his father replied.

"Want to go now. Want to see the jaff and the tiger!"

"You have to help me in the garden."

Emer breathed a sigh of relief. She could slip away to the school. "I have to collect my bicycle from the school, Dad."

"Bring some tea and toast up to your mother first, will you?"

"Did we wake her too?"

"No, she's been awake for a long time." He looked out the kitchen window far into the distance.

"Is she—getting better?" Emer asked hesitantly.

"We hope so. We hope so." Her father's voice was not convincing. "Now bring her the tea and toast."

Emer availed of the opportunity to toast an extra few slices of bread.

Her mother was sitting up in bed when Emer brought

17

in the tray. She smiled weakly, smoothed the coverlet and invited her daughter to sit beside her. "Now tell me all about yesterday!"

Emer recounted all the adventures of the day—all except the one she longed to tell. Her mother particularly enjoyed the stories about Josie Byrne and Emer's attempts to mimic Miss Dunne's voice. It was good to see her mother laugh. For a moment Emer was tempted to confide in her.

"Mum?"

"Yes."

Emer suddenly noticed how quickly the colour had drained from her mother's face. "I—I have to collect my bike from the school. Is that all right?"

"Of course."

Emer decided to take the short-cut across the fields to the school. Apart from saving time, it was a way of avoiding any of her friends.

"Bring me back the paper from Rigney's," her father called from the vegetable garden. She waved in acknowledgement.

"And bring me a tiger," Johnny called.

Emer's heart beat excitedly as the school came into view. She sat for a moment atop the gate to get her breath back. She would have a long chat with Duck. What a silly name! And if he once mentioned the word "redneck"— she clutched the plastic bag tightly until she realised she was mashing the toast.

"Breakfast is—" The words died suddenly as she rounded the corner of the bicycle shed. She instantly knew there was no one about. She called out his name, feeling silly as she did so. He was gone. She circled the school building, just in case, but he was gone. There was

18

worse to come. Her bike was gone too. Then she remembered her anorak. She would have some explaining to do now. That was bad enough. She could rightly claim they had been stolen. What hurt her most was his lack of trust, his downright ingratitude. She had risked getting into trouble. She had taken him on trust. Trust. He probably couldn't even spell the word. He was obviously more of a criminal than he had admitted. Emer was furious. She felt like flinging the food at two crows that sat on the school railing, but instead she used it as a punchbag to ease her frustration.

She went home by the roads. It didn't matter if she met anyone now and anyway she had to call in to Rigney's shop for the paper.

"How is your mum?" Mrs Rigney asked.

"She's in good form." She's not going to be in very good form when she hears my anorak and bike are gone, Emer thought.

"Ah, the summer will bring her on, please God."

Emer shoved the paper into her punchbag and strode home, grim-faced. I hate people who cheat, she thought. I hate people who let you down. A warm sun beat down on her. She spoke to no one but kept her eyes fixed on the road. She welcomed the shade of the huge oak trees that towered over the wall of Dunrickard House. When she came out into the sun again, a distant glint caught her eye. It came from the chapel. The chapel was a small private church, now unused, which stood in the grounds of the Dunrickard estate. The glint came from the sunlight playing on the handlebars of a bike. Her bike. She clambered over the wall and raced across the field.

The door of the chapel was slightly ajar. She eased herself in. The chapel was unfurnished except for a couple of broken pews ranged along one wall. Along the opposite wall ran a series of huge stone vaults. Although there was a welcoming coolness inside the chapel, Emer felt uneasy there.

"D-duck!" she called timidly. She jumped as a flutter of wings in the rafters above her head answered her call. She shrieked as the door shut behind her and a voice said, "Breakfast is late!"

There stood Duck, dripping wet, smiling at her. He was wearing only a pair of cut-off jeans. She stared at him, fuming. "What's the matter?" he asked.

"You—you stole my bike—and my anorak."

"No I didn't—they're both here. Your bike's punctured though. Sorry about that."

"Oh, so that foiled your escape—"

"No it didn't. Will you cool down?"

"No I won't. You told me you'd be in the bicycle shed. You told me to bring breakfast—"

"Yeh. Where is it? I'm starving."

She flung the bag at him.

"Temper! Temper!" He rooted in the bag and began eating hurriedly. "Sausages are cold but they'll do. Don't suppose you brought anything to drink?"

She glared at him for a moment. "Where's my anorak? I'm going home."

"Look, will you sit down over there and I'll explain."

"There's nothing—"

"Sit down!" he barked. She backed away in fear and sat on a broken pew.

"Now," he began, relishing the last sausage. "All that happened was that I couldn't sleep in that shed. Couldn't get comfortable. So I left in the middle of the night—on your bike—and rode till I saw this place. Didn't know it was a church until I broke in—"

"You broke in?"

"Of course. It was the butler's night off! Anyway. Dead cool, isn't it? *Dead* cool—do you get it?" He gestured towards the vaults.

"And where were you just now when I came in?"

"Went for a swim. Saw the lake when I woke this morning and couldn't resist it."

"But you'll be seen—"

"But I wasn't! Don't worry. I'm good at hiding." There was a silence as he waited for her next charge. Emer looked away in embarrassment. He searched for the last crumb of toast.

"I still think you were leaving," she said at last. "It was only by accident I saw—"

"I would have found you. I would have brought your bike back."

"Where?"

"To school—on Monday."

"You wouldn't come to the school—"

"Why not? Don't I know most of your class—not to mention Frosty-face? Ah go on, smile! Your face won't crack. Thanks for the breakfast. You can keep the paper!" He handed her the newspaper in the plastic bag.

"I can't do this everyday. They'd notice at home."

"You don't have to. I'll be fine once I've sussed the place out."

"What will you do—steal food?" she asked sarcastically.

"'Course."

"But it's wrong—to steal."

"Wrong? What's wrong about it? If you have nothing and you want to stay alive, you go out and get it. Right?"

"No. Wrong!"

"Ahh!" He kicked an imaginary obstacle out of his way and hauled himself up on top of a vault. "Goody-goody! You don't know what it is to be hungry—"

"Yes I do!"

"I mean really hungry. A day—or days—without food."

"Why didn't you ask?"

"Ask! Ask who? All I'd get would be a kick out the door. When you're on the street, no one wants to know—"

"On the street?"

"Yeh, homeless. Sleeping in doorways, boxes, that kind of stuff."

Emer looked directly at him. He looked like a bird perched on the edge of the vault.

"Tell me your story," she said quietly.

Chapter 4

Duck's Story

"I told you my story already!" Duck swung his legs impatiently against the vault.

"That was in about half a minute. Take a bit longer this time!" Emer teased.

Duck squinted at her to avoid a shaft of sunlight that played on his face. "You're a funny one," he said. "I feel like I'm on the bleedin' stage here," he added, sidling along the edge of the vault to get out of the way of the sun that was spotlighting him. Emer smiled but said nothing.

"OK," he sighed. "Born on the 4th of July 1981 in Dublin. Me da was from Nigeria—studying to be a doctor. I don't remember him. He went back to Nigeria when he qualified. Left me nothing but his name. Me ma was—is—Maureen Kelly. She got sick when I was a baby. I was put in care."

"What's that?"

"In a home. In a cot, really. I still remember that cot. The paint was gone off the bars. I remember the bars—gripping them and bawling. I remember the nurse having an awful job getting my hands away from the bars. Anyway, me ma got better—for a while—and she took me out. We lived in a flat. She had lots of boyfriends. Most of them didn't like me. So I was out on the street from an early age. You learn to look after yourself."

"How about school?"

"What do you think? I spent most of the time outside the door, or in the principal's office. They all picked on me. They'd say things about me or me ma, so I hit back at them. Or else I mitched. Went on the run. Down the town. Usually had my dinner in Moore Street."

"Moore Street?"

"Yeh. The fruit-stalls. Into the odd shop for a packet of biscuits or a bar."

"Were you not caught?"

"Sometimes. The guards would just bring me down to the station, or back to school. Until the next time."

"And what about your mother?"

"She didn't care. Then she started on the drugs. Selling them. She was nicked for that and put in jail."

"And you?"

"I was put into St Mark's. A 'home for disturbed children' they called it. The staff were more disturbed than we were. The boss was mad. We called him Groucho—Mark's. Groucho, get it?"

Emer nodded with a smile.

"Every morning he was grouching about something. Usually a little thing, but he'd make a big thing out of it. Like one morning he came in and roared, 'There are two stoppers missing from the hand-basins in the washroom! I want to know what happened to them!' So I said to McCormack beside me, 'I told you those mushrooms were tough last night—'"

Emer spluttered a laugh.

"I was on toilet duty for a week."

"What was that?"

"Keeping the toilets clean."

"What else did you do out there?"

"We had school. Well, sort of school. There was Harpic—"

"Harpic?"

"Yeh. 'Cos he drove us round the bend. He tried to teach us English and stuff. He'd have debates which always turned into rows. And there was Sawdust—he did woodwork, when he wasn't putting his arm around you. I threatened him with a chisel one day, so he left me alone. I was no good at woodwork anyway. The pieces never fitted. The only class I liked was Jo Jo's. He was an old brother who used to work in the garden. I liked being in the garden—making things grow. Then Jo Jo got sick and there was no more gardening. Someone broke a window and I got another week's toilet duty. That's when I decided to get out. So I got on your bus and ended up in the wild west. Redneck country!" Emer bristled at that word.

There was a long silence. Duck swung his legs up on top of the vault and stretched out full-length on the slab. "What about you?" he asked eventually.

"What about me?"

"How many jails have you been in? How many murders have you committed?"

"None—yet!"

"Is that a threat?"

"Not really."

"Well—what's your story?"

"A boring one I'm afraid. My dad drives a lorry. We live about a mile from here. Dad, Mam, Marion—she's fifteen and thinks she's the most important person in the world—me and Johnny. He's four and he's a handful when I have to mind him, which is a lot because my mam isn't well, hasn't been for months."

"What's wrong with her?"

"Not sure. Some problem with her blood. She keeps having tests—" Emer's voice was suddenly drowned by a loud whirring noise in the field outside. The noise grew louder as it gradually approached the chapel. There was a startled look in Duck's eyes as he dived for cover between two vaults.

Emer scurried to the door and peered through the crack where the shaft of sunlight shone through. "It's all right," she whispered. "It's only Paddy Power cutting thistles." Above the din they could hear Paddy singing at the top of his voice.

"He sounds like the Terminator. Will he be back?"

"He'll be up and down the field for a while, so you'd better stay where you are." Emer glanced at her watch. "Jiminy! It's after twelve, I'll be murdered!" She grabbed the newspaper and eased the door ajar, before turning back to Duck. "I'll see you tomorrow—if you're still here."

"I'll probably be in the local hotel."

Her voice took on a more serious tone. "You'll have to think hard about what you're going to do. You can't hide in buses and churches all the time."

"Look. For you it's hiding. For me it's freedom. And I'm going to enjoy it. OK?"

"OK." She felt chastened. "Goodbye."

"See ya. Thanks for the breakfast."

Paddy Power was at the other side of the chapel and heading down the field. She slung the plastic bag over the handlebars of her bike and wheeled the bike smartly towards the open gate.

The excuse of a punctured bike did little to explain Emer's late arrival satisfactorily. "Did you go to Galway for the paper?" her father asked drily.

"And there's no bread for my breakfast, greedy pig," Marion whined.

"Oh Emer, what were you doing?" her father snapped, holding up a grease-stained newspaper.

The sausages. The toast.

"Don't know," Emer lied. "Mrs Rigney must have—"

"And mam was looking for you. I suppose I'll have to study on an empty stomach," Marion sighed.

"When are we going to see the jaff, Emer?" Johnny asked.

Emer had had enough questions. She darted from the kitchen to her bedroom and flopped on to her bed. Ever since she had met Duck, she had had to lie her way out of trouble. Maybe he just was trouble. What he was doing was crazy anyway. He couldn't keep on the run forever. Especially someone who was—black. Maybe he would move on again tonight. Maybe he would just give himself up. That would be best really. Really? To go back to Groucho—and Harpic—and toilet duty? She clambered across the bed and reached into the top shelf of her wardrobe. She withdrew a jar with a screw-top lid. The educational tour had depleted her savings considerably, but she still had six pounds, fifty pence. She slid the money under her pillow and smiled to herself. It would buy him some time.

They passed by the chapel on their way to and from Sunday mass in her father's car but there was no sign of life in the little stone building. Emer wondered how he had slept there. It wouldn't be her favourite place to spend a night, in among the vaults.

The day dragged by. Emer had to help with the dinner and the washing-up and then play with Johnny before she could even think of slipping away. She smuggled a leg of chicken from the fridge before announcing her departure.

"I'd like to go and see Laura," she said, trying to sound as casual as possible.

"I'll give you a lift," her father replied. "The minor hurlers are playing this evening. I want to see if they're any good."

Emer would have to see Laura now, whether she had intended it or not. The Dalys lived just beyond the village, quite close to the hurling pitch.

"Don't be all evening," Marion called after her. "I've got study to do and I'm under enough stress without Johnny annoying me!"

Laura was sitting up watching television when Emer arrived. Her arm was in plaster and her pale face was cut around the nose and forehead. Emer was genuinely taken aback by her friend's appearance, but Laura dismissed it readily. "You should see the other guy!" she boasted.

"What other guy?" Emer asked innocently.

"That was a joke, Emer. Lighten up! And where's my stick of Dublin rock?"

"I'm sorry. I forgot—"

"Well at least give me all the news!"

Emer recalled as much of the day as she could, especially the adventures of Josie Byrne. She longed to tell her friend all the news—but the time wasn't right, yet. "Now, what on earth happened you?"

Laura recounted the details of her accident and her time in hospital.

"Poor you!" Emer sighed as she signed her name on Laura's plaster.

"Yeh! I lay there on Friday morning feeling all sore and sorry thinking of you on your way to Dublin, you lucky duck!"

"What?" Emer was startled by the word, causing the pen to become embedded in the plaster.

"Emer Healy, what is the matter with you? You're like a hen on a hot griddle for the last while."

"I'm sorry. I have to meet someone—"

"Your boyfriend?"

Emer blushed. "Very funny! My dad!" *There I go lying again!*

"Well don't let me keep you," Laura said tetchily.

"It's not that. My bike is punctured, so if I miss my lift, I'll have to walk home." *That's not a lie....*

"OK." Laura smiled. "When will I see you again?"

"After school, some evening this week."

"See you!"

Emer made her way down through the village to Rigney's shop. She spent three pounds buying a selection of food for Duck—cheese singles, crackers, fruit, biscuits, crisps and a three-litre bottle of orange—"special value at 99p!"

"There must be a party going on somewhere." Mrs Rigney's curiosity was blatant.

"Sort of," Emer laughed as she dashed out the door. She looked anxiously about before crossing the field to the chapel. Any onlooker who might notice a girl with a bulky bag of shopping entering the chapel on a Sunday afternoon would be immediately suspicious and that would put Duck in danger. There was no sign of life in Power's, the nearest house.

Emer moved quickly along the hedge and then cut across to the chapel. She prised open the heavy door and called out "It's me!" in a loud whisper. There was no reply except for the rapid fluttering of wings up in the roof. She jumped back, startled, then called again, edging her way inside. He was gone! Again! That was twice he had done that. Why? She propped the shopping bag on top of a vault and stretched her aching fingers. Why did I bother? He doesn't care about anything. She ambled around the chapel, half-hoping to see a note pinned to one of the pews. There was nothing. Emer sighed and picked up the bag. Better find an excuse for a party at home....

Once again she surveyed the scene from the doorway. Not that it mattered if she was seen now. The strong evening sun had turned Lough Finn into a pool of silver. She moved towards the road and then hesitated. On an impulse she doubled back and headed for the lake. The lake waters lapped quietly around the stones that dotted its edge. The sheen from the surface was dazzling. Emer slipped off her sandals, sat on a large rock and trailed her feet in the delicious cool water.

"Dinner is late!" The voice, although familiar, startled her so much that she almost toppled into the water. He was no more than ten yards away stretched out lazily on a bed of dried reeds. Emer glared at him. "I knew you'd find me," he said. "What's for dinner?"

"You could have left a note," she growled. "I didn't find you! I just came down here by accident. You seem to think, you seem to think—" She shook her head, lost for words.

"Do I take it," Duck affected a posh accent, "that you are upset that I was not at home when you called?"

"Yes," Emer mumbled, tightening her grip on the bag. She knew that once he started acting like this, she could no longer be angry with him.

"Well it was such a lovely afternoon," he continued. "I gave my staff the day off and went for a walk around the estate. Don't you think my lake is looking well?"

30

"It's our lake, and here's your dinner," Emer said offering him the leg of chicken wrapped in foil.

"Oh good—is that it?" He gave the drumstick a puzzled look before chomping it greedily.

"No it isn't. Just be patient!" She began handing him her purchases, one by one.

His eyes lit up with delight. "Did you nick these? Well done!"

"No I did not nick them. We're not like that—" she checked herself, drew a deep breath and continued slowly. "I bought them with my own money."

"You—with your own money. Why did you do that?"

"I'm beginning to wonder why myself."

There was a hiss as he opened the bottle of orange. He took a long, long drink and offered Emer the bottle. "Do you want a swig?"

She shook her head.

He munched an apple. "An apple?"

Another shake of the head.

"Well what would you like?" he asked, with slight annoyance.

"A 'thank you' would be nice. I went to a lot of trouble—"

"You didn't have to!" He jumped up and kicked the apple core into the water.

"No, I didn't—that's why a 'thank you' would be—"

"OK. Thank you! Thank you! Thank you! Is that enough?" he roared.

Emer had had enough. She began to put on her sandals hurriedly. She felt foolish hopping around on one foot while trying to pull a sandal onto the other.

"OK! OK!" Duck said quietly, digging his toe into the mud at the water's edge. "I'm sorry. It's just that I've had enough of being told what to say. 'Say please'—thump! 'Say you're sorry'—thump! 'Say thank you'—thump!"

"No one's thumping you now."

"No." He looked at her and laughed. "Would you ever sit down? You're like a one-legged crow there!"

Emer gave an embarrassed smile and sat back on a rock. Duck looked intently at her. "You're OK. You know that?"

"Of course I know it." They both laughed.

"This is great," Duck said as he stuffed the food into his hold-all.

"What have you got in that bag?" asked Emer.

"Just things, my things," Duck replied.

Emer understood from the tone of his voice that he didn't want the topic pursued. "You can't go on like this much longer," she said firmly, looking across the lake.

"Like what?"

"Living in a chapel. And I've only got a few pounds—"

"It's all right. I'm sussing things out. I'll be moving on soon."

"Where?"

"If I knew, I'd tell you!" He offered her a bag of crisps. She took a few crisps and they munched in an uneasy silence. Suddenly Emer remembered something. She searched in the plastic bag.

"More food?" Duck teased.

"No. Something I brought to help you pass the time. There!" She held out a paperback book to him.

"A book? What would I want with that?"

"It's brilliant! *The Secret of Seven Oaks.*"

"I don't want to know the bleeding secret of Seven Oaks or Six Oaks, or Five Oaks."

32

"But it's a great story. You'd—"

"I don't want it, OK?"

"OK." Emer was hurt again. "I just thought it would help—"

"Well it wouldn't!"

"Why?"

He picked up a stone and threw it as far as he could into the water. "Because—" He threw another stone. "Because I can't read—that's why!" The stone plopped loudly into the water.

Chapter 5

The Reading Lesson

Miss Dunne was droning on in class. "Now, children, what is the poet trying to tell us here? He's telling us that life is short for daffodils—

> *Fair Daffodils, we weep to see*
> *You haste away so soon*

and maybe life is short for us too...."

"You can't read?" Emer had asked in disbelief.

"No. Well I was out of school more than I was in it, wasn't I? And when I was in it, nobody bothered because I was so far behind."

"So you can read something?"

"Oh yeh, I know my letters and 'Run Pat run'. That wouldn't get me far!"

"Well it's a start. I'll teach you to read," Emer announced with pride.

"You? How could you?"

"You'll see! I teach Johnny things!"

"Yeh, but he's clever. I'm stupid!"

"Who says?"

"Teacher, Groucho, Harpic—the lot of them."

"They're the stupid ones. They probably never tried

very hard. Just leave it to me!" She felt confident.

"Well I'd rather have you than old Frosty-face!"

"Maybe you'd like to read it for us, Emer?"

"What?"

"I beg you pardon, teacher. Not 'what?'" Miss Dunne corrected her. "I suggested you might like to read for us when you wake from your dream!"

"Oh. Yes, Miss. Fair Daffodils, we weep—" She was interrupted by titters from around the classroom.

"I'm afraid we left the daffodils about ten minutes ago, Emer. We're on to the story now. But as you're so fond of the daffodils, perhaps you would write the poem out three times tonight—"

There was a snort of laughter from Jenny Gavin.

"And Jenny can do likewise. Three times please, Jenny!"

"Ah, Miss—"

"Four times!"

Emer looked up from her homework to watch the rain sweeping across the garden. Even if she hadn't so much to do, she couldn't go to see Duck in that weather! The mood in the house reflected the weather. Her father was fixing her bike in the kitchen. He was depressed by the defeat of the Tubberfinn minor hurlers the previous day. "Not enough commitment," he muttered to himself. "Never get anywhere without the commitment. Only the under-14s left now." Every summer Kevin Healy lived in hope that a hurling team from Tubberfinn would achieve glory, but every year it was the same pitiful story.

Marion was in a sulk because her French teacher had said she didn't know why on earth Marion was doing

35

Higher Course French in the Junior Cert Exam.

"I hate daffodils," Emer muttered as she started to write the poem out for the third time.

"Are there daff-dils in the Zoo, Emer?" Johnny called from under the table where he had chased his racing car.

"Sometimes Johnny, sometimes."

Emer had just finished her homework when her mother called her to the bedroom. She hated the frailty of her mother's voice. She hated even more the weakness of her smile. She remembered that when she had been Johnny's age, her mother would swing her up high in her strong arms, her voice strong and reassuring, her face alight with laughter. Why can't now be like then? Emer wondered. Why do things have to change?

"I've tried reading the paper, but I'm just too tired. Would you read me the headlines, love?" her mother asked. Emer nestled at the foot of the bed and scanned the headlines.

RACIAL TENSION IN LOS ANGELES
TYRONE BUILDER SHOT DEAD
MANY FEARED LOST IN BANGLADESH FLOOD
THREAT OF ANOTHER FAMINE IN SUDAN

"Isn't it a sad world we live in?" her mother sighed. "Look inside and see if you can find any good news."

Emer turned to the fashion page. "Paris says yes to flares as the 70s come back in vogue," Emer read. Her mother laughed quite heartily. "We'll have to go through the wardrobe, Emer. I may still be in fashion—"

Emer, however, was no longer listening. Her eye had caught a single item under the heading "News in Brief"—

BOY MISSING

Martin Oduki (12) has been reported missing from St Mark's Care Centre in Dublin. Martin, who is black, was last seen on Thursday last, wearing a navy tracksuit and blue runners. Any information concerning his whereabouts should be forwarded to St Mark's or to any Garda station—

"Emer?" The voice was weak again. "Emer, you're in a dream!"

"Sorry, mam. I just got interested in something else."

"What was that?"

"A missing boy—it's just a story."

Fortunately for Emer, her mother's tiredness was rapidly overcoming her. "Just read me the cartoons and give me a laugh."

Later that night when Johnny was fast asleep, Emer switched on her reading light and took a bundle of well-thumbed books from her locker. She examined the titles in the "Well-Loved Stories" series.

The Little Red Hen, *The Ugly Duckling*,—no, not yet, she smiled—*The Little Porridge Pot*—Johnny's favourite—*The Three Little Pigs*—she would start with that.

"*The Three Little Pigs*! I'm not reading that! That's only for babies!" Duck waved the book away with indignation.

"It's only for people starting to read. Just give it a try. You'll probably fly through it."

"You're just laughing at me," Duck said with genuine embarrassment.

"No I'm not. I just want to help, that's all. Now come on. Let's give it a try."

He sat reluctantly beside her on the broken pew. Emer read slowly, tracing the words with her finger. Duck sighed with boredom at first but gradually took a greater interest. Emer read through the whole story and then, to her amazement, he interrupted her on the second reading. "Wrong! It's 'bricks!'" he corrected her.

"Pardon?"

"That word, it's 'bricks'. You said 'brick'."

"How did you know that?"

"I didn't. I just know if there's an 's' at the end, it must be 'bricks', not 'brick'."

"Very good," Emer beamed. They had made a start.

"You sound just like Frosty-face!" he teased.

When they had finished the lesson, Emer rooted in her school-bag and produced a pencil and jotter. "I'll leave these with you. You could practise some writing—just copying words out of the book."

"Is that my homework?"

"Yes, and if you don't do it, you'll have to do it three times the next day. That's what Frost—what Miss Dunne would do!"

"No bleedin' way!"

"Oh, by the way—there's something else," Emer said casually. She held out the newspaper cutting.

"I can't read that!"

"I bet you can read bits of it!"

He stared intently at the scrap of paper. "Hey—that's

me! That's my name. I'm in the paper. And—St Mark's, Dublin." His face lit up on recognising the words.

"I told you you could read some of it!"

"But what does it say?"

"It says, 'Boy Missing.'" She pointed to the words and read the full item.

"So, I'm famous! It's time to move on!"

"No. You're in no danger around here. What's the food situation?"

"OK. I'm making it last."

Emer delved into her school-bag again. "Here. I made a double helping of sandwiches for lunch!"

"Thanks!" He wolfed down the sandwiches and reached into his hold-all for the bottle of orange.

"I have to go. Have to collect Johnny. Promise me two things. Don't be in a hurry to move and do your homework!"

He made a playful face at her.

"Bye!" She whispered, peering to see if the coast was clear. She noticed some movement at Power's, but decided to take a chance.

"See you!" Duck laughed. "By the way. You—are—a—brick!" He spoke slowly in his best "teacher's" voice.

Emer collected Johnny from Mrs Kenny's playgroup on her way home. She was pleased with herself, with the way the reading lesson had gone. She could teach Duck. She knew that. It wasn't like teaching Johnny. She could teach Duck—if only he stayed around long enough.

"Emer, I saw a jaff today," Johnny chirped as he swung out of her hand. Not again, Emer thought.

"Mrs Kenny had a big picture, bigger than me! When are we going to the Zoo, Emer?"

"Don't know, Johnny. Maybe—"

The moment they rounded the bend, she sensed there was something wrong—even before she saw the ambulance parked in their gateway. She grabbed Johnny's hand tightly and ran.

"It's only to do more tests, love. It won't be for long." Her mother took Emer's hand in hers—a hand that felt cold and limp to Emer's touch.

Johnny nestled on the pillow beside his mother. "Can I go in the am-blance?" he asked.

"Not this time, Johnny." She cradled her son for a minute. "You have to help Emer mind the house and Auntie Breda will be coming to see you."

"Will Brian be coming too?"

"I'm sure he will."

"Oh goody." He slid off the bed and ran down to his father. "Daddy, Brian is coming to play with me."

Emer fought back the tears as she watched her father cover his face with one hand and give a strange sigh. He drove off after the ambulance. Emer watched until the ambulance disappeared around the bend in the road. Then, leaving Johnny to watch television, she ran to her bedroom, flopped on to her bed and, clutching her favourite teddy tightly, cried softly for the next fifteen minutes.

Marion arrived home from school in a foul humour. "Typical, just typical," she barked to no one and every-one, tossing her school-bag against the fridge. "Shane Joyce was at the Blazes Disco on Saturday night and was asking all night for me. And where was I? Baby-sitting you two! Typical!"

"Mammy went off in the am-blance," Johnny announced, but Marion ignored him.

"Not burgers again," she scoffed as she opened the

oven warming drawer.

"Mammy's gone to hospital," Emer repeated Johnny's message.

"Oh, for what?"

"More tests, she says."

Marion pulled her chair in to the table and paused before eating. "How long will she be away?"

"Don't know."

"Well I hope it's not for too long. My exams start in a couple of weeks—"

"God, Marion, do you ever think of anyone but yourself?" Emer shouted at her sister and ran from the kitchen. Marion froze for a moment, holding knife and fork in mid-air, her puzzled gaze following Emer out of the room. Wiping a few tears from her eyes, she noticed she wasn't hungry any more.

There was a buzz in Emer's classroom the next morning. She felt that she was being excluded from whatever the source of the excitement was, but she was too preoccupied with other things to find out why. Her father didn't want to talk about her mother's condition, her sister was still in a huff and, as if he sensed the atmosphere about him, Johnny was particularly cranky when she had left him with Mrs Kenny that morning. Emer had had little time to think about Duck but he was brought abruptly into her thoughts in a most unexpected way.

"Miss! Miss!" Paula Power clamoured for attention after roll-call.

"Yes, Paula," Miss Dunne answered in a tired voice.

"Miss, my brother Liam saw a blackie yesterday!"

"A blackie?"

"Yes, Miss. A black boy!"

41

"A nig-nog!" "A woggie!" Two anonymous comments from the back of the class brought nervous titters from the other children.

Miss Dunne glowered at them. "Stop that! I'll have none of that talk in this classroom!" There was a momentary silence. "Now, Paula, what is this nonsense all about?"

"It's not nonsense, Miss. Liam was pucking a ball around the Chapel Field when he saw this black boy dart out of the chapel and off through the fields like a hare. He got a terrible fright, Miss!"

"I'm sure he did, Paula. Liam always did have a lively imagination—"

"But Miss—"

"Homework, children, quickly!"

Emer's heart raced at the news. Her face burned. She felt she was blushing so obviously that the whole class would notice. She buried her head in her school-bag while rummaging for her homework. She struggled through the morning, wondering all the time if what Paula had said was true and, if so, what had happened to Duck. Every time Emer stole a glance at Paula, she found Paula staring at her. She must know, Emer thought. She must.

Her suspicions were confirmed at lunch-break when Paula approached her in the yard. "My mammy's nearly sure she saw you coming out of the chapel the other day," Paula said with a suspicious look.

"What would I be doing there?" Emer laughed nervously. "I'd be terrified of going there!" She felt her face burning again.

"Maybe not if there was a blackie there!" There were shrieks of laughter from the knot of girls that had grown

42

around Paula. Emer was in a corner. The only way out was to fight.

"You and Billy Gavin should know what it's like inside the chapel anyway."

A chorus of jeers arose from the group. Paula was riled. "Billy Gavin? I wouldn't be seen dead with him."

"Especially in a vault!" someone shouted from the fringe of the group, to the amusement of all.

"What's wrong with Billy Gavin?" An angry voice stilled the laughter. It was Jenny, Billy's sister. There was an uneasy silence.

"N-nothing," Paula stammered. "He's just—not my type, that's all!" There were more jeers, followed by further jibes about the Power and Gavin families. Emer felt awkward about having started the row, but relieved that it had deflected attention from her. There was further relief afforded by the school bell. Lunchtime was over.

Emer found it difficult to concentrate on the afternoon's lessons. She would have to warn Duck if it wasn't already too late. But how to get to him when she knew that she was under suspicion? Fortune favoured her when Mrs Kelly, the infants' teacher, announced that there would be camogie practice after school. That would keep Paula Power out of the way for a while.

Emer was first out of school when classes finished and was racing away on her bike before any of her classmates had time to notice. She rode past the Powers' house and past the Chapel Field before hiding her bike in the next field. Emer crept back towards the chapel, keeping it between her and the Powers' house. She watched carefully to see if there was any movement, then took a deep breath and darted around the building.

From the moment Emer hurriedly forced the door open, she knew that Duck was gone. She could sense the emptiness of the place. Her disappointment at his absence was eased by the relief that he had, with luck, escaped the prying eyes of the Powers. She took a second, more careful, look around. Her eyes fell on a wad of paper wedged in the ornate carving at the end of a broken pew. She hastily unfolded it. The message, scrawled unevenly and obviously hastily in pencil on a copybook page, was still very clear:

Boy Missing
The House of Straw

Chapter 6

Escape!

Duck had not slept so well for a week. The hay was warm and welcoming. He had wrapped himself in a musty cocoon of it, with just his head and arms protruding. He had been awakened by the noisy patter of jackdaws walking on the iron roof just above his head. Duck shook the cocoon away, lay flat on his back and reflected on the happenings of the previous twenty-four hours.

A different noise had awakened him on what proved to be his last morning in the chapel: a dull thud against the chapel door; the sound of whistling and footsteps approaching. Duck wedged himself between a vault and the wall and froze. The footsteps retreated again. He breathed out slowly. The pattern was repeated. The thud. The whistle and the footsteps. The footsteps retreating.

Duck crept quickly to the door and peered out. The lumbering figure of a tall, stockily built boy, trailing a hurley behind him, loomed threateningly ten metres away. He walked on, turned, tossed the hurling ball in the air and struck it with all his might. Duck winced as the ball cannoned off the metal door behind which he was hiding. His heart pounded as he dared to peep out at this intruder into his world. He noticed a shock of red hair dancing above a freckled face, but it was the look on that face and the arrogant saunter of the boy that made Duck even more uneasy. This boy knew something. He wasn't there just to practise his hurling. Duck sat with his back to the door. He was trapped. He held his breath as the footsteps approached. There was a mocking tone in the whistle. Once again the footsteps retreated. A pause. Thud! It was a cat and mouse game. The redheaded boy was stalking his prey, waiting for Duck to make a move.

Duck crept back to the vault, opened his hold-all and hastily tore a page from Emer's copybook. He opened *The Three Little Pigs*, unfolded the newspaper cutting about him and hastily copied a message for Emer.

Thud! He waited, then hid the message in the pew. He crept back to the door clutching his hold-all. He would simply have to make a run for it and hope for the best. His best chance would be when the boy's back was turned. He peered out. Too late this time. The boy was about to strike the ball. Duck closed his eyes, awaiting the thud. It never came. Instead there was a loud oath from the boy as the ball soared above the door, hit the roof, spun upwards and trickled down the other side of the chapel. This was Duck's chance. He waited as the muttering boy went in search of the ball.

Duck slipped out and stole along the chapel wall, around the corner and along the end wall. The redheaded boy was poking among nettles with his hurley, occasionally taking a wild swipe which cut a swathe through the nettles. Now! Duck hopped across to the hedge. If he could get through to the other side, he would have cover. He found a gap and wriggled through the hedge. A twig snapped under his foot. The redhead looked up, caught a glimpse of Duck disappearing through the hedge, gave a wild throaty roar and took off in pursuit. The chase was on.

46

Duck wrapped the straps of his hold-all around his arm and flew straight down the field towards the lake. His pursuer, though much bigger than Duck, had an awkward gait and often floundered in the long grass and nettles that grew along the hedge. He made an attempt to burst through the hedge but became entangled in briars and roared in pain.

Duck reached the lake and veered left along the water's edge, weaving his way through the tall reeds. Behind him he heard the boy swearing as he stumbled again. Duck paused in a nest of reeds to catch his breath. His last glimpse of the boy was of a frustrated figure, madly flailing at the bramble hedge with his hurley. Duck smiled and went on his way. He knew exactly where he was heading. He'd been on a scouting mission the previous day. He reflected that, careful though he had been, the redheaded boy had probably seen him then.

Duck followed the lake-edge for another half-mile, then turned away to rising ground through a strange wood and then downhill again. He followed a narrow road, keeping to the fields, until the road eventually petered out into a rough gravel track. The land on either side of the track was very low-lying. He followed the track through rushy fields until once again the ground began to rise. He made his way through a pine copse and there it stood before him—a neat whitewashed house. It was small, one-storeyed, though Duck had noticed a tiny window high in one gable. He kept well clear of the front of the house, moving in a wide arc through the pine trees to the back.

Some distance from the house there was a cluster of outhouses. One of these was well packed with hay. Duck stole in and clambered his way to the top. He sank into the comfort and musty warmth of the hay, still clutching his hold-all. He was asleep in spite of himself within minutes.

Duck chewed on a stem of hay and reflected on his fortune so far. He had been lucky in meeting Emer. He hoped she would find his note. He had been lucky in escaping from the redheaded boy and he had been lucky in finding this place. It was isolated from other houses and, though he had not seen its occupants, there was a welcoming air about the place—something he couldn't explain but could definitely feel.

A loud rumble from his stomach woke him from his reverie. He could not remember how long it had been since he had eaten, but he was starving now. He reached for his hold-all. There were only scraps of food left. Suddenly a low vicious growl came from below. Duck felt the hair tingling along the back of his head. He remained motionless but the growling continued, rising in pitch all the time. There was a shuffling noise as the door creaked open. A voice called softly, "Is there someone there?" Duck remained silent. "Down, Scutch. Down!" The voice was firmer. "Is there anyone there?" Duck said nothing but turned very slowly towards the voice and opened a peephole in the hay with his fingers. Slowly the slightly bent figure of a man came into view. To Duck he looked old, leaning heavily on a stick. The man spoke to the dog again and turned to go. As he made his way out of the shed, Duck realised that it wasn't his age or his bent figure that caused him to shuffle. He was feeling his way along with the stick. The man was blind.

Luck was staying with the fugitive—but so was the dog. Duck couldn't see it but the growling continued below him. The man turned, slapped his stick against his boot and called impatiently. "Come on, Scutch. Come on out of that!" Duck lay back with relief. Another problem overcome—for the moment. He searched in his hold-all for food. A few biscuits remained, soft and tasteless. His stomach was still rumbling. He would have to go in search of food. Maybe Emer would— a low growl came from below. That dog again. A voice spoke to the dog. A different voice. There was a pause and then— "Come on down from there, whoever you are!" It was a woman's voice. Another pause. "Come on. And if you try any tricks, I have a dog and a pitchfork here that you'll answer to!"

There was a sharpness in the woman's voice that commanded respect. Duck looked about him. There was no other way out. He would have to face the woman. He rose slowly in his hay-nest to a kneeling position. The woman stood in a defensive pose, clutching the pitchfork tightly. When she saw the black face of a young boy emerge above her, a great change came over her. "Glory be to God!" she whispered, casting the pitchfork aside and giving the growling dog a kick. "Be quiet, Scutch!" she muttered. "Come on down, child. He won't harm you— and neither will I!"

Duck slithered down the hay, landing directly in front of the woman. He could have made a dash for freedom but the woman's gaze was almost hypnotic. She was of slim build, her white hair swept back from the lined, weather-beaten face that had seen many years of toil. But it was the bright blue eyes that transfixed the boy before her. As they faced each other, a kindly smile transformed her face and tears welled into her eyes. "Glory be to God!" she whispered again, her eyes now watering openly. "You're a home child, aren't you?" she said softly.

"A what?" Duck queried, half-embarrassed, half-puzzled by the woman's reaction to him.

"A home child. You've come from a home, an institution. I can see it in your eyes."

Duck shrugged his shoulders. The woman wiped her eyes with the back of her hand, wiped her hands in her apron and tentatively reached out to place her hands on the boy's shoulders. "You need have no fear in this place. We will look after you. I can see that you're hungry too. Come, child. Come and eat. You're with friends now." She offered her hand to him. Duck saw his own hand take hers, almost as if it were not part of him. She grasped it warmly and led the boy from the shed into the bright daylight outside, across a little paddock and into the kitchen of the thatched house.

The kitchen was cool and welcoming. "Sit down there, child, and I'll get you something to eat." Duck sat in a chair by the fire. A big black kettle hung on a crook over the fire and droned away happily. Duck surveyed his surroundings. A huge dresser ran along one wall, laden with an assortment of china and crockery. An old television set sat on a window-sill. The woman worked away in one corner, moving between a small fridge and a gas cooker. She sang quietly to herself as she stood over the cooker, stealing an occasional glance at the boy.

The delicious smells coming from the cooker were almost overpowering. Duck tried to distract himself by observing his surroundings even more closely. An alarm clock ticked away on the mantel over the fireplace, and affixed to the chimney-breast was a very ancient-looking hurley, blackened by years of soot and smoke. Two hens appeared in the doorway, cackling softly.

"Shoo!" the woman cried. "Can't you see I have a visitor?" There was delight in her voice.

At last she summoned Duck to the table and placed before him the biggest fry he had ever seen—rashers, sausages, pudding and two fried eggs.

"Eat now, child" she said, putting a pot of tea in front of him. "Eat now. We can talk later."

Duck savoured every delicious mouthful. It was his first proper meal in over a week. He ate quickly and with relish. When he stole a glance at the woman, she simply urged him to continue eating. He soaked up the last of the fried eggs with a piece of delicious home-made bread, chasing every last crumb around the plate. "That was lovely," he said at last.

"You needed it and you enjoyed it," the woman replied. "Now—if you feel like talking, tell me what brings you to the Island."

"The Island?"

"Yes. Come the winter, we're almost cut off here. The water comes all around us. But what about you?"

Duck sat back in the chair. For the second time in a week, he told his story to a complete stranger. He told it because she had won his confidence in the way she spoke to him, in the way she understood his needs, but above all in the way she looked at him. She never interrupted as he spoke, occasionally nodding in support of what he said. He finished his story.

"And what is your name, child?"

"Martin." He would keep the rest in reserve for the moment.

"Well, Martin, it's a familiar story you tell," she sighed. "I know it all too well. You see forty years ago I was in the same position. I was a home child too."

51

Chapter 7

Granny's Story

"Well not exactly a home child, though in truth I wasn't much more than a child." The woman sat down at the other end of the table from Duck, cradling a cup of tea in her hands.

"It was forty years ago, forty-two to be exact. I was nineteen years old and I fell in love with Eddie Browne. A grand boy he was, not much older than myself. Too much in love we were and before we knew it there was a baby on the way—and that was the end of Eddie and me."

"Why?"

"You wouldn't understand, child. It was the 1950s. It was the Dark Ages. You didn't do things like that. Not like now—nobody would bother much if it happened today. But then—it was the worst thing in the world. Do you understand, child?"

"Sort of. You could have got married, couldn't you?"

The woman laughed softly as she shook her head. "Indeed not. We had sinned, so we had to be punished. I was read off the altar."

"What's that?"

"I was publicly accused and condemned at Sunday mass by a Canon who was nearly ninety years old."

"And what happened to Eddie?" The boy's interest in the story grew as his appetite for food was satiated.

"Eddie was despatched to England. To Birmingham,

where an uncle found him a job. He settled there. I heard he met another girl, married her and had a family." She took a long drink from her cup of tea. "I hope he's happy," she sighed.

"And you? What happened to you and the baby?"

"I was sent to the Magdalen." She looked away through the little kitchen window.

"What's the Magdalen?"

"It was a laundry in Galway run by the nuns—and it was a home for bad girls like me."

"But you weren't bad—"

"No, child. But in everyone else's eyes I was. I was an outsider like yourself."

"I know the feeling," Duck said resignedly. "What was it like in the home?"

"'Twas like what it was—a prison. You were watched all the time. Never trusted. Every door was locked behind you. And you worked so hard." She looked away again. "So hard. Scrubbing, wringing, carrying—in the steamy heat. And all the time the baby was growing inside you. And all the time nobody came." Her voice trembled and grew hoarse. "Nobody. And nobody cared."

"And the baby?" Duck asked.

"Edward was born on 21st March at five past four in the afternoon. He weighed seven pounds twelve ounces—and he was a beautiful creature." Her eyes began to mist over. "I had him for three days. Three days. Then they took him away for adoption. I never saw him again. But someday I might. I pray every night for that to happen. He's a man in his forties now, but I still have hopes...."

"And did you—could you leave the home then?"

"I couldn't—but I did! Just like you. For once a door wasn't locked. I took a chance. It was fair day in Galway.

I got a lift out of there and ended up here. Well, in this area. I was lucky to find a job in Dunrickard House—cleaning and laundry and things. I was good at laundry!" She smiled for the first time since she had started her story. "They treated me well. That was the main thing. I was a person again. And then—years later—I met Tom."

"That's the blind man?"

She nodded. "Poor Tom. He was the local blacksmith. Lost one eye in an accident in the forge. Then the other one started to go about five years ago. But he manages very well. He knows every inch of the place. Together we manage. We haven't much but we have enough. And what we have is yours, Martin, for as long as you want."

"Thanks." He was surprised at being addressed by his proper Christian name. "I—I don't know your name," he said.

The woman laughed heartily. "Amn't I the poor hostess? Never introduced myself! Nan Flynn—though everyone calls me Granny Flynn. I don't know why. Tom and I were never blessed with children." She sighed again. "Aye! That's the way life goes."

"What about Tom? Will he not mind me staying here?"

"Not when I tell him your story. He'll understand. He knows my story." She looked at Duck thoughtfully for a long time, then nodded to herself, having made a decision.

"Come with me. I have something to show you." She beckoned to him to follow her through a dark cool parlour which was evidently little used. In the corner of the parlour a narrow stairs ascended steeply. Granny led the way up the stairs and opened a door at the top. Duck found himself in a cosy little bedroom, sparsely furnished but bathed in warm sunlight which filtered in through the window he had noticed earlier in the gable end of the house. What surprised him most was that the room was ready to be occupied, as if a guest was expected.

Granny Flynn looked approvingly around the room and beamed at Duck. "This can be your room," she said gently.

"No. No. The hayshed is fine. I slept like a log there." He was clearly embarrassed.

Granny shook her head. "I know people would think me crazy if they knew about this—but you're the first to know about it anyway. For thirty years I've kept this room like this—ready. Ready for the day Edward would walk in the door below. Now—" she placed a hand on Duck's shoulder, "now I think maybe Edward has come home after all...."

Duck shrugged his shoulders. He didn't know what to say, but he strolled around the room, touching the sloping ceiling beams. He came to the window and peered out. "Oh good, you've got a garden!" He could see Tom on his knees tending to some vegetables.

"There's many a sighted man would be proud to have Tom's garden. Do you like gardening?"

"It was the only thing I liked at St Mark's."

"Well there you are. You'll be a great help to Tom— for as long as you want to stay, that is. You're free to come and go as you please, Martin. There's never a lock put on a door in this house, day or night." They exchanged knowing glances. "I'll leave you to yourself now," Granny said, retreating to the stairs. "If there's anything you want, ask, and if we have it, it will be yours."

Duck pushed his hold-all under the bed and lay back, resting his head on his cupped hands. How lucky he had been in his choice of refuge. To think he had chosen the house of someone who had had a similar experience to himself. He closed his eyes, a smile of contentment on his face. He was asleep almost instantly.

He awoke to the sound of voices downstairs. It took a few minutes to accustom himself to his new surroundings. He did not know how long he had slept but he had slept very deeply. He listened. There were only two voices—Tom and Granny. He came downstairs, deliberately stepping on the squeaky step he had noticed on the way up.

"Here he is now. I've just been telling Tom all about you. Tom, this is Martin." Tom turned away from the fire where he had been lighting a pipe. His kindly sightless face wore a broad smile as he extended a hand in welcome.

"Good man, Máirtín." Another variation in the name. He shook Duck's hand vigorously. "You have a strong wrist. Did you ever hurl? We could do with a forward—"

"Will you leave the child alone, Tom?" Granny gently scolded her husband. "You've no sooner met him than you have him in the hurling team! This man lives for hurling, Martin," she explained, gesturing to the blackened hurling-stick hanging on the mantel over the fireplace. "I'll leave ye to talk about something while I get the tea."

"What time is it?" Duck asked.

"Just after six o'clock. You slept well!" Tom gestured towards the television set on the window-sill. "Switch on the news, Máirtín, like a good lad." As he listened to the news he nodded or shook his head, drawing occasionally on his pipe. "'Tis a quare old world, Máirtín. Shooting

56

and bombing and robbing is all that makes the news now." Duck mumbled in agreement. "You're doing a bit of travelling yourself?"

"A bit, yeh."

"That's good. They say travel broadens the mind." No more was said about Duck's situation. They talked about vegetables, about the Island and about Tubberfinn until the subject of hurling came up again. "We'll have to teach you to hurl," Tom said with enthusiasm. "'Tis a mighty game!"

"You played a bit yourself," Duck replied, eyeing the hurley on the chimney-breast.

"Oh you noticed! 1949—Tubberfinn were county champions. Never before and never since. Aye and never again at the rate the young lads are leaving nowadays! We were a mighty team. I played centrefield—with the 'Thresher' Larkin. The paper said we were 'majestic'. I have it somewhere. Aye. 'Majestic'." He drew on his pipe again. Granny called them to the table.

"Is he replaying that match again for you?" she asked.

"'Tis worth replaying!" the old man countered.

"Let the child eat in peace, now."

After tea they watched television for a while, until Tom suddenly asked, "Do you play draughts, Máirtín?"

"Yeh! We used to play it a lot in St Mark's."

"Oh you'll regret you said that," Granny warned. Tom was already reaching into an alcove to his right, from which he produced a battered biscuit tin. He prised the lid off to reveal a set of well-worn draughts.

"I have to play him every night," Granny explained. "He says he's the champion, but I did beat him once!"

"Arra that was the day that old billygoat strayed into the yard and the smell of him distracted me," Tom argued as he set up the board.

"But how can you play?" Duck began. Granny silenced him by putting a finger to her lips and showing him one of the black draughts. It had a little niche cut in the edge. Each black draught had a similar cut.

"Now, Máirtín, I'll give you a crack at the title!" Tom said, rubbing his hands at the prospect of a new challenge.

Duck played his best, moving cautiously, but Tom eventually trapped two of his kings and the game was over.

"I'm still the champ!" he chuckled.

"Can I have another go?" Duck asked, confident that once he had become familiar again with the game, he would beat the old man. The second game lasted an even shorter time.

"Hee! Hee!" the old man chortled, "the champ still reigns!" He was thrilled at having met and resisted the new challenge. "I'll give you another crack at the title tomorrow night!"

"I'll be ready, champ," Duck laughed.

Duck went to bed that night with a light heart. He slid between the cool starched sheets and gazed out the little window at the still bright sky. For the first time in many nights he would sleep without having to watch out or to feel he was being watched.

He reached into his hold-all and took out a small framed photograph. He looked at it for a long time—the girl cradling a tiny black infant in her arms. She would be about nineteen too, he thought. He slid the photograph back into the hold-all, turned over and fell into a deep sleep.

Chapter 8

Robbery!

E mer followed her father nervously down the hospital ward past whispering groups gathered round each bed. There were screens around her mother's bed. When they sidled through a gap in the screens, Emer was shocked by her mother's appearance. She seemed to have shrunk since Emer had last seen her. Her eyes had retreated into a face that was waxen and wan. Her mother's voice was hoarse and frail.

Emer fought back the tears as she kissed and hugged her mother. She tried desperately hard to sound cheerful as she related Johnny's latest antics or the funny words he used and also Marion's continued complaints that no one understood how much she was suffering from examination stress. In reality everything was a blur. Emer kept wishing this was all a bad dream from which she was about to wake. She withdrew to the foot of the bed to allow her parents to have a private conversation.

Her father told her the news when they got into the car. "It's a tumour," he said quietly. "She'll have an operation on Saturday. We'll just have to hope and pray," he added with a sigh, squeezing Emer's hand so tightly that it hurt. There was no further conversation on the journey home. Emer forced herself to think about Duck, if only to get her mind off her mother's operation. Where was he?

She thought again of his message, "The house of straw." He obviously meant a thatched house—but which one? There were quite a few of them in the neighbourhood. Her father slowed down as he passed a woman wheeling a bike with a full shopping-bag on the handlebar. It was Granny Flynn. The moment Emer saw her a warm feeling came over her. She knew that Granny Flynn's thatched house on the Island had to be the "house of straw".

Emer hurried through her chores and played with Johnny until Aunt Breda arrived. "I'm just going to visit a friend," she explained as she mounted her bike.

"Dinner will be at seven. Don't be late!" her aunt called after her.

Emer sped towards Tubberfinn before turning down a back road which would lead her to the Island. This road would also take her away from the prying eyes of Paula Power, who still teased her at school about her black boyfriend. "How's the Blackie?" she would taunt. "Heard ye were at the pictures in Galway!" Emer ignored her, hoping that Paula would soon tire of the teasing and turn her attention to someone else.

As her bicycle bumped along the rough track, she wondered why Duck had chosen this place as a refuge and for how long he could go on hiding. She found the answers to her questions within minutes of arriving at the little thatched house. Granny Flynn came out to greet her, dusting flour from her hands. "You must be Emer— and you're looking for Martin."

Emer had to think for a moment about the name. "Y-yes" she stammered. "Is he—"

"He's told me a lot about you, how kind you were to

60

him. It's important for people to be kind to someone who's had a tough time."

Emer looked at the ground in embarrassment.

"He's not here," the woman continued. She noticed the immediate look of disappointment on Emer's face. "But if you cut across through the wood, you may find him over at the lake."

"Thanks!" Emer shouted as she dashed away, only to cannon into Blind Tom who came around the gable end of the house at that moment. She mumbled an apology and kept going. She had only been in the wood once before. Her father had told her it was called the "Witches' Wood" but he could not remember why. "No time for witches now," Emer thought as she waded through the ferns to the top of the little wood-covered hill and then down again to the lakeshore.

She noticed Duck sitting on a boulder at the water's edge. His back was to her. Emer was about to call out a friendly greeting to him when she observed that he was gesturing to someone else. Puzzled, she crept out of the wood, through the tall grass and closer to the boy. Now she could see the object of his attention. Two swans were riding the lapping lake waters about twenty metres from where Duck sat. As Emer crept nearer, she could hear a single voice. It was Duck's voice and he was clearly talking to the swans.

Emer felt she should not interrupt. She strained to catch Duck's words. "...envy you two. I really do. No one pushes you around. You can go where you want. Stop where you like, for as long as you like. You're free. All you have to do is flap your wings." He bent down to pick up a pebble and threw it towards the swans. There was a tremendous splashing and flapping as the swans

61

suddenly took off and soared over the wood. Emer watched in awe as the swans passed directly over her head, legs tucked neatly under their bodies, their mighty wings whirring and swishing in unison.

"What did you do that for?" she called, half in anger, half in puzzlement.

"What?"

"Scare them away like that?"

"Just wanted to see them fly."

"But they mightn't come back now."

"They'll come back—if they want to!"

"Not if people throw stones at them." Emer had by now reached the boulder on which Duck was sitting. He stared at her, his eyes narrowing in anger.

"Look, I just threw a pebble at them to make them fly. Big deal! Are you going to have me arrested for that?"

Emer looked away to the lapping water. Why was he so touchy? She was beginning to regret that she had come.

"I like swans. They're big and they're free—and they're white!" He threw a fistful of pebbles viciously at the water. "In fact, I wouldn't mind being a bleedin' swan!"

Emer took a deep breath. "Well you know what happened to the Ugly Duckling...." she said. There was a long pause before Duck eventually smiled sheepishly.

"What kept you?" he asked.

"Couldn't make out your mystery message!"

"Clever, wasn't it?"

"Except there are loads of 'houses of straw' around here."

"Yeh, but...."

The ice was broken. They were at ease with each other

again. They exchanged their stories. Duck told of his escape from Liam Power and his meeting with Granny Flynn. Emer related Paula Power's taunting and her mother's impending operation.

"Are you worried about it?"

"Of course. Don't want to think about it. I have to mind Johnny all day Saturday. Marion's staying overnight in Galway. Big revision for her exam, she says. Big pyjama party if you ask me!"

"Why don't you bring Johnny down here?"

"Could I? You don't think Granny would mind?"

"'Course not!" They had started walking back through the wood. "Tom is dead cool for a blind man," Duck said suddenly. "Do you know he beats me at draughts every night? And he says he'll train me to be a hurler. And him blind! Haven't got a hurley anyway," he laughed.

"I know. We can borrow Marion's, she used to play camogie—"

"What's that?"

"It's a sort of hurling for girls. Anyway, now that she's studying so hard, she has no time for it. I'll bring it on—"

Duck grabbed her by the shoulder and pulled her behind a tree.

"What—?" she began.

He motioned to her not to speak and pointed towards the house. There was a large blue van parked at the gable end.

"Do you recognise it?" he whispered.

She shook her head.

"There's something funny going on. I can smell trouble from here," Duck said. "Come on!" He moved swiftly from tree to tree. Emer shadowed him until they reached the outhouse where Duck had hidden on his first day there. They could hear voices through the open kitchen window. They were not friendly voices. Duck indicated that he was going to investigate. He crept around in an arc in the shelter of the outhouses, disappearing from Emer's view until he suddenly appeared at the back wall of the house. He dropped on all fours, scuttled along to the open window and listened. Emer watched anxiously for some indication of what was going on.

Duck's heart pounded as he heard a man's voice rasping through the window above his head. It was cold, measured and threatening. "Come on now. You must have some old stuff in a place like this. We'll pay well." The voice ranged from one side of the kitchen to the other as the man paced to and fro.

"We only have what you see." It was Granny's voice, almost a whisper but determined. "We have nothing to sell. You came to the wrong house."

There was a long pause, then a scraping noise. Duck was growing frantic. He threw a puzzled look in Emer's direction and slowly edged his eyes above the window-sill. A burly figure leaned against the inside of the window, almost obliterating his view. He peered through the small gap to the right of the figure and saw two things which told him enough about what was happening. In the dim light he could see the terror in Tom's sightless eyes as the old man hunched in his chair by the fireside. In front of Tom, Duck could see a huge hand wielding a long black tongs and scraping it noisily along the hearth. The intruder's voice spoke again, louder and more menacing. "So maybe you have some cash hidden away here, eh?"

Duck dropped his head below the window. His throat felt dry and dusty. He wanted to scream in anger but he realised that might only put the old couple in further danger. He would have to divert the men's attention. The van! He crept along the gable end of the house and padded across to the van. The key was still in the ignition. Good. That would make things easier. Even better was what lay on the passenger seat. A mobile telephone! He reached in, grabbed the phone and retreated in the cover of the van to the outhouse. He handed the phone to Emer. "Quick! Ring the guards! There's a pair of gougers in there trying to rob Granny and Tom! Quick!"

"I—I don't know how—" Emer stammered. Duck grabbed the phone, switched it on and dialled 999. He thrust the phone back into Emer's hand. "Tell them where we are—and tell them to be quick!"

He was gone again before she could reply. He shot across to the van, opened the passenger door and slid across to the driver's seat. He took a big breath and turned on the ignition. The engine shuddered into action. Duck rammed the gear lever down into second gear and practically stood on the accelerator. The van shot forward across the paddock and down the incline towards the track that led from the Island. Above the noise of the engine he heard someone shouting in the distance. He glanced in the wing mirror and saw two figures waving their arms furiously and beginning to give chase.

Duck allowed himself the briefest of smiles before concentrating on what lay ahead. What he was about to do looked exciting and easy when he had seen it in a movie, but now he was terrified. He had a fleeting memory of Tom's face and the scraping tongs, then he gritted his teeth and aimed the van at a little abutment halfway down the track. He held the steering wheel firmly with his left hand while opening the door with his right. The van was devouring the track now and, as it mounted the abutment, Duck pushed the door wide open and jumped.

For a few seconds he felt himself floating and tumbling in space. He then hit the ground hard. Fortunately he landed on a mound of moss and rolled down into waterlogged rushes. He was dazed but unhurt. He looked around hurriedly. The two men were charging down the track, screaming foul abuse at him. He glanced towards the van. It had landed upright but was sinking steadily in the ooze. The wheels had almost disappeared. Duck gave a shout of triumph and took off across the marsh, hopping nimbly from mound to mound. He had reached the safety of the tall reeds by the time the men got to the van. He flung himself on the reeds and looked back at the comical scene that was unfolding.

The men had waded to the van and were trying desperately to open the doors. They swore in frustration, banging on the sides of the van. They then turned on each other, each obviously blaming the other for their misfortune. Duck lay among the reeds, enjoying the scene immensely. The two men were still arguing when the blue flashing light of a police car appeared over the brow of the hill and bore down on the hapless stranded pair.

Chapter 9

A Day Out

Everything had happened at such a bewildering pace. The events of the previous hour had left Emer both excited and confused. The guards had arrested the two robbers and had taken statements from Emer, Granny and Tom. The old couple were shaken but relieved that things had turned out all right.

"Those two lads have been the scourge of old people in the West for the past few months," the senior garda told Emer. "We've been looking for them for a few weeks now and here they are, trapped by a slip of a girl! You're a very brave young lady!"

Emer looked away in embarrassment. What else could she have done? Duck had disappeared. She presumed he didn't want to become involved with the guards, so she told them that she had simply let off the handbrake and the van had rolled down the steep incline and into the marsh. The robbers knew otherwise but they were so furious and ashamed at being caught through the actions of a young boy that they said nothing.

When the two had been taken away in the patrol car, Emer scanned the horizon for a sign of Duck. "He'll lie low for a while," Granny said, noticing Emer's anxiety.

"But why?" the girl asked. "It was he who had the men

caught. He got me to ring the guards—"

"Ringing them was one thing. Facing them is another," Granny said with a knowing look. "He'll come back in his own time."

Emer cycled home slowly. Her mind was in turmoil—the excitement of the robbers' arrest! What would she do when word got out, as it surely would, that she was a "heroine"? Where was Duck and when would he come back? Behind all those thoughts was the one she could not banish—her mother's operation. She was rudely awoken from her reverie as she approached the house.

"Practising for the slow bicycle race, I suppose?" It was the cynical voice of her sister. Marion was stretched on a sun-chair, surrounded by an array of sun-creams, soft drinks and snacks. The tinny sound of a driving beat rang through the headphones of her Walkman. She sipped from a can of orange and peered over her sunglasses at Emer.

"Here am I struggling with my French verbs and trying to keep Johnny out of my hair while you're gadding around the countryside...."

Emer walked past her. "Hmph!" Marion snorted, retrieving her book of French verbs from under the chair. "*Je faillirai*—I will fail," she barked. "*Tu failliras*—you will fail."

There was a strange atmosphere in the Healy household on the next Saturday morning. Emer's father was unusually quiet and when he did speak he tended to snap at everyone, even Johnny. Marion announced that she was going in to Galway "to do some last minute group study," and would take a lift with her father who was driving to the hospital. Group study in Supermac's or Eyre Square, Emer thought.

"What are your plans?" her father enquired.

"I'm taking Johnny to a friend's house," she replied hastily, hoping there would be no further questions.

"Can we go to the Zoo, Emer?" Johnny asked. "I want to see the jaff."

Emer ruffled his blonde hair. "Not today, Johnny. But I know where there are swans."

"Well let all of ye say a prayer," her father cleared his throat nervously, "that things will go well today."

"Oh look," Marion said pointing at the fine drizzle that had begun to fall. "*Il pleut!* How can I study in that?" Definitely Supermac's, Emer thought.

Her father glowered at Marion. "Come on if you're coming at all!"

The drizzle had given way to hazy sunshine when Emer set out on her journey for the Island. She took out her mother's bicycle, partly so that she could feel a little closer to her mother on this day, but also for the practical reason that it had a baby seat on the carrier. Johnny just about fitted into the seat and, with a basket swinging from the handlebars and a hurley attached to the frame, Emer set off somewhat precariously on her journey. It was a difficult push all the way, made more difficult by Johnny's endless questions about all he saw around him. Emer was breathless when she finally dismounted to wheel the bike along the rough track to the Island.

Scutch came yapping to greet them as Granny Flynn peered cautiously over the half-door. "He's away" she said quietly.

"He's—gone?" Emer's heart sank.

"No, love. It's just that he's being cautious since the other day. He came back late last night and left early this morning."

"I think I know where to find him. We're going to have a picnic."

"And who is this big man?"

"That's Johnny, my little brother. Say hello, Johnny."

"Hello! Have you any jaffs?" The woman looked puzzled.

"Don't mind him," Emer laughed. "Ever since I went to Dublin Zoo, he has me tormented about giraffes!"

"Well I have no giraffes, but I'll have something nice for you when you come back."

Emer and Johnny wound their way up the hill and through the wood. The tall pines offered them welcome shade from the oppressive heat. Johnny insisted on collecting pine-cones and loaded the basket further. When they reached the summit, he careered down the other side, often tumbling in the carpet of pine-needles. Emer envied him as she struggled behind with the basket. They reached the clearing.

Emer scanned the lakeshore for the swans. They were not immediately visible but she eventually caught sight of a white shape bobbing about in a tiny sheltered cove. She headed for the cove, urging Johnny to go quietly so as not to scare the swans. Duck was hunched on a flat rock, tossing pieces of bread to the swans.

"Hi!" Emer called nervously.

"Big birds!" Johnny shouted.

The startled swans raised their wings. Duck motioned to Emer to stay back and be quiet. She took Johnny into the withering reeds and waited until Duck had finished feeding the birds. They bowed their heads as if in gratitude and glided gracefully away from the shore.

"That's amazing!" Emer said, "I never knew swans would come that close to you."

70

"I had to talk to them for a long time first. Action Man here nearly spoiled everything," he said, making a playful dive towards Johnny.

"Sorry about that. This is Johnny. Johnny, this is Duck."

"No, *they* are duck," Johnny said, pointing to the retreating swans.

"They are swans, silly," Emer laughed. "I brought a picnic," she added quickly, tumbling out the pine-cones and reaching into the basket for food. She noticed Duck moving about with some difficulty. "Are you all right?"

"Yeh—just a bit sore after the other day."

"What happened? I couldn't see—"

"Nothing much. I just did like they do in the movies—jumped out of the van before it landed in the bog."

"Are you sure you're all right?"

"Yeh. Just stiff." He shrugged his shoulders in the comical kind of way that Emer had grown accustomed to by now. Johnny was playing with his pine-cones.

"You were very brave—and I got all the praise."

"If there's a reward, we'll split it!" he said, chewing on a broken reed. Emer poured drinks for the three of them and opened some packets of crisps. They heard a distant rumble of thunder as they drank and munched.

"Better eat up quickly, guys," Emer warned. "There's rain on the way." The two boys paid little heed to her. Duck had joined Johnny in building a pine-cone castle. Emer had no option but to join them. She procured two tall green reeds to act as flags for the castle.

"I'm king!" Johnny announced.

Duck saluted him as he burrowed an approach road to the castle.

71

Without warning, the heavens opened and huge raindrops slapped their faces. "I told you! I told you!" Emer screamed as she gathered up the picnic things.

"It's only a bit of rain," Duck said calmly.

"My castle. Want to bring my castle!" Johnny shouted.

"Oh come on, Johnny. Don't mind your castle," Emer snapped.

"No! Want my cones!"

Duck scooped the pine-cones into Emer's basket, swept Johnny up on his shoulders, took the basket in his hand and set off for the wood with a wild whoop. Emer laughed as she followed the wild horse and its chuckling rider. The wood afforded them some shelter, but Duck continued careering through the trees in zig-zag fashion as Johnny clung to him, shrieking each time they took a sharp turn.

"Well, glory be! What kind of circus is this?" cried an amused Granny as the breathless trio crowded noisily through the cottage door.

When they had composed themselves, they became aware of the delicious smell that was wafting across the kitchen. Granny had spent the morning baking. An array of cakes, from tiny fairy cakes to a large tart, sat cooling on a shelf by the cooker.

"I suppose ye have no appetite for food after the picnic," Granny teased, noticing the longing looks they cast towards the shelf. She paused for a moment, then heaped a variety of cakes on a plate and put it before them. "But just in case—"

They needed no more bidding and began an assault on the plate, savouring the exquisite freshness of the confections before them. Granny placed a large bottle of fizzy orange and three glasses on the table. The three exchanged looks of sheer pleasure as they ate and drank without interruption.

Tom came shuffling in from the rain, a sack draped around his shoulders and Scutch bouncing excitedly in front of him. "God bless the work!" he called. Emer looked around the kitchen. Tom sat in his chair by the fire, cradling a steaming mug of tea that Granny had produced. Granny scurried busily to and fro attending to everyone, her round face beaming with happiness. Scutch sat expectantly beside Duck, hoping for a treat.

We're like an instant family, Emer thought—as if Granny and Tom had adopted us all.

"Now, you'll have to leave a bit of room for this!" Granny announced proudly, placing a steaming-hot rhubarb tart in front of them. "This is Tom's favourite!"

"'Twill keep ye going till you get a bite," Tom chuckled. Granny cut the tart in portions and drenched each portion with cream. The aroma of the tart was simply luscious. Each of the three scraped their bowls clean. Johnny began to lick his bowl.

"Johnny, don't do that!" Emer cried in embarrassment.

"Mammy lets me lick," Johnny retorted.

Mammy! The word sent a cold quiver through Emer's body. She had forgotten. How easily she had forgotten. She felt guilty. Suddenly it wasn't right to be having fun when her mother was.... She rubbed away the tears that welled in her eyes. She was aware that Duck was watching her.

"I have a surprise for you!" he said and went bounding up the stairs to his room. He was back again almost immediately clutching his copy-book. "There!" he said, proudly opening it before Emer. He had copied the entire story of *The Three Little Pigs* in his own writing and went on to read it to an enthralled Johnny.

"Brilliant!" Emer clapped her hands in delight. "Told you you could read! Which reminds me; I've got a surprise for you too!" She delved into her basket and took out a brightly illustrated book.

"It's *Willie the Wimp*!" Johnny cried in delight.

"This is Johnny's favourite book, and we're going to read it to you!" Emer read the story while Johnny pretended to read by tracing his finger along the words. "Will you give Duck a loan of your book, Johnny?" Emer asked. Johnny nodded.

"Did you ever see the 'Rabbit in the Hole'?" Tom enquired. The three shook their heads. Tom proceeded to play a finger game in which his index finger popped up as a rabbit and then magically disappeared into a burrow of fingers. The three were spellbound by the old man's sleight of hand. They stared in silence as the rain cascaded off the thatch outside. "Do it again!" Johnny called impatiently each time Tom had finished.

"Come on, Johnny," Duck intervened, reaching for the basket of pine-cones. "Let's build our castle again." The two of them began building on the kitchen floor, but they had not got very far when Scutch ruined their plans by running off with one of the cones, causing the castle to fall apart.

Johnny laughed hysterically. Scutch's antics soon became a game, a matter of how much the two boys could build before the dog darted in and snatched a cone away. Emer watched Granny wipe away tears of laughter with her apron and clap her hands in delight. It was such a happy day, if only.... Emer wondered about her mother. Was it over yet? Was she in pain? Thinking of her mother, she wished the day were done. Hearing the laughter all about her, she wished it would never end.

The rain finally stopped and a watery sun enticed them out once again. Emer suddenly remembered the other surprise she had brought. The hurley was still tied to the frame of her bike. "It's Marion's, but she hasn't used it for ages—she's been studying so hard!" she added cynically. "And there's an old hurling ball, which I also—borrowed!"

"Good," said Tom. "We'll make a hurler of you now, and no mistake."

Duck looked bemused and poked awkwardly at the ball until Tom took the boy's hands in his and showed him how to grip the hurley. "'Tis all in the wrists. That's the secret!" he whispered. "And you have good strong wrists." Duck noticed how strong the old man's wrists were. "Now try a few swipes!"

Duck began awkwardly, conscious of how many pairs of eyes were watching him. He missed a few strokes at first but gradually he developed a rhythm and made contact each time.

"That's it!" Tom nodded. "You're getting there. Now I want to hear that ball meeting the middle of the boss...."

"The boss?"

"The head of the stick, boy. There's no sweeter sound than the leather on the middle of the boss." The lesson continued, with Emer and Johnny retrieving the ball from the other end of the paddock. "Now I'll test you," Tom challenged. "There's a barrel outside the hayshed. I want you to hit the bottom of it."

Duck measured the distance with his eye and struck the ball. He gave a whoop as the ball slapped against the barrel.

"Not good enough." Tom shook his head. "You hit the top of the barrel."

"But—"

"'Tis half full of water. I know by the sound." Granny gave a little chuckle. "Practice. That's all you need," Tom laughed. "But you made a good start."

Emer cycled home with a light heart. What could have been a long day of worry had turned out to be a fun day, thanks mainly to Duck. The basket of pine-cones bounced off her knee. Her back-seat passenger was strangely quiet. As they turned the corner to their own house, he spoke at last.

"Emer," he yawned.

"Yes."

"Can we go to see Duck again?"

"Hope so," Emer smiled to herself. It made a change from giraffes.

Chapter 10

The Secret Exposed

E mer was first home. She put the exhausted Johnny to bed. He was asleep before she had crept out of the room. Now that she was alone in the quiet of the evening, her worries about her mother returned. She sat by the window, waiting anxiously for sight of her father's car. The warm evening sun beat in on her. She felt drowsy herself after the day's excitement and was just about to nod off when the car swung into the driveway. Emer opened the door in anticipation of hearing good news.

Marion brushed past her, giving her sister a vicious look. Her father followed, looking very troubled. Emer's heart pounded. It couldn't be—

"W-well?" she stammered.

"Well what?" her father snapped.

"Mam. The operation. How did it...."

"It went OK. We'll just have to wait and hope." There was a long pause. He wasn't very pleased, even if the operation had gone well. Then it came.

"You never told us you were a big hero," Marion sneered.

"I'll deal with this, Marion," her father said, waving the elder girl away. He turned to Emer. "It seems you were up to all sorts of adventures, but your own family are the last to hear about them."

"I couldn't tell you. There's a reason...."

"Well, you'll have to tell me now. The whole village is talking about it. For a start, what were you doing there anyway?"

Emer sighed. She was trapped. She would have to tell the whole story. Marion hovered behind her father, wearing a broad smirk on her face. Emer took a deep breath and told the story of Duck from the day of the school tour to the wonderful day she and Johnny had just spent at Granny Flynn's. There was a long silence when she had finished.

"You were taking a lot of chances there, young lady," her father said at last. "Marion, put the kettle on, will you?" he added quickly. Marion glowered at her father and dashed out to the kitchen.

"Not really," Emer said nervously. "Duck is very nice when you get to know him."

"But how well do you know him? He's been in a lot of trouble. In fact trouble seems to follow him—"

"But if he hadn't been there, Granny and Tom would have been robbed. They could have been beaten up, or maybe even murdered."

"He put you in danger."

"I was in no danger. The robbers didn't know I was there."

"A fellow like him is very...unsettled. You should stay away from him."

"I don't want to stay away from him. He's my friend—and he hasn't many friends."

"You'll stay away from him, is that clear?"

"But he was brilliant with Johnny today."

"No, Emer."

"And Tom's teaching him to hurl. You could put him

78

on the under-14s—"

"Emer, I've had a long and tiring day. Your mother's very ill. I have enough problems without you hanging around with a...." He paused.

"With a runaway? Is that the problem?" Emer was surprised to hear those words come from her own mouth.

"That's enough out of you, lassie. Get up to bed out of my sight!" He turned and stomped into the kitchen. Emer was left standing in the hallway on her own. Tears welled up in her eyes. She went quietly to her room, lay on her bed and cried herself to sleep.

Emer would have preferred to stay in bed all day Sunday—away from prying eyes and whispered comments—but her father had everyone up in good time for eleven o'clock mass. Emer felt that every pair of eyes in the church was fixed on her and she shuffled about awkwardly while her father chatted with friends in the churchyard after mass. Please let nobody come up to me, she prayed. Please....

"Hi Emer!" a voice called. Emer's heart sank. This was the start of it. She turned around with a sigh. To her delight it was Laura Daly.

"Laura! It's great to see you!"

"It's my first day out. I feel a bit wobbly!" Laura leaned against a car, awaiting her parents. Emer's genuine pleasure at seeing her pal up and about again was multiplied when it became clear that Laura had not yet heard of the incident on the Island. They chatted excitedly until her parents arrived and they parted promising to meet again soon.

Emer's heart was lighter on the journey home, even though Johnny was the only one to break the uneasy silence with his non-stop chatter. "When we going to see Duck again, Emer?" he asked suddenly.

"Don't know," Emer replied cautiously. "Maybe he's gone back to Dublin."

"Is that where the jaffs are?"

"Yes!" Emer growled playfully. Would he ever forget about the giraffes, she wondered. And when would she see Duck again? She would have to explain why she had exposed the secret.... The car passed by the Powers' house. Paula stood outside and gave a cheery wave. Emer's heart sank again. School. She would have to face the music there.

The "music" was even worse than she had feared. Emer deliberately took her time going to school, hoping to avoid questions in the yard. She arrived just as the last line was entering the school. There was instant silence when she entered the room. Miss Dunne, taken aback by the sudden absence of the usual chatter, peered over her glasses and smiled on recognising the reason for the hush.

"All right, children," she chirped. "I think we should greet our local hero, or should I say heroine, in the proper manner!" She stood up, beaming proudly and began clapping vigorously. The children quickly joined in, adding whoops and cheers. Emer felt her cheeks burn with embarrassment as she slid into her seat. Miss Dunne quelled the growing din with difficulty. "Enough! Enough, children—please! Josie Byrne, get down off that desk at once!" Finally in desperation she slammed the roll-book against her desk. The startled children fell silent.

"Really children. Manners, respect—and dignity!" She waved away a cloud of chalk-dust which the roll-book had showered into her face. "Now I think," she coughed as the dust enveloped her, "I think our heroine should tell us her exciting story of courage, don't you children?" There was a mighty cheer of approval, which led to a chant of "E-mer! E-mer!"

Emer looked appealingly to her teacher, her eyes asking to be relieved of this embarrassment, but Miss Dunne only beckoned to her to stand before the class. No way, Emer thought. She gave a long sigh and stood up. The children fell silent again.

"I—I just want to say," she fought against the increasing dryness in her throat. "I just want to say that I had little or no part in the capture of robbers at all. It was Duck—"

"Duck?" A chorus of bafflement arose from the children.

"He's a boy who's—"she paused nervously, "on holidays around here." There were titters and giggles around the classroom. From the corner of her eye, Emer saw Paula Power nudge the girl next to her.

"Yes Paula, you were right," Emer said. "I'm sorry, but Duck didn't really want to meet anyone. He's—shy." More giggles. "His name is Martin Oduki but everyone calls him 'Duck'."

There was a brief silence until "Biffo" Power, seated at the back of the classroom, put his hand to his mouth and went, "Quack! Quack! Quack!" A couple of his pals in the back bench took up the call amid growing laughter. Emer slid back into her seat as a flustered Miss Dunne clapped her hands furiously and tried to restore order. "Children! Children! Manners! Respect! Dignity!"

It wasn't until she had put Biffo Power and James Burke standing outside in the corridor that quiet returned to the classroom. Emer opened a book and buried her head in her hands. She had done it. Duck would never forgive her. And she couldn't get to him to explain. He would probably move on now.

Duck stood up from the drill and stretched backwards. He had been weeding the vegetable garden and his back ached all over. He surveyed his morning's work with satisfaction, then made his way to the paddock and retrieved the hurley stick and ball from the hayshed. He began practising some of the strokes which Blind Tom had taught him. Lift the ball cleanly from the ground with the hurley and drive it hard against the bottom of the barrel or lob it gently onto the roof of the hayshed and wait for it to drop down before volleying it against the barrel. Such was his concentration, he failed to notice two figures making their way along the track to the Island. Scutch did notice them, however, and began to bark excitedly.

Duck watched their approach with some anxiety. They were young, about his own age. Each carried a hurley. There was something familiar about one of them— the stocky build and, as he came nearer, the tousled red hair and the freckled face. It was the boy who had discovered him in the chapel. The two strutted to within ten metres of Duck, then paused. Duck stood his ground, bouncing the ball on his hurley.

"Howya, Blackie?" the redheaded boy taunted.

"Howya, Quackie?" the other echoed.

"Howya, Duckie?"

"Howya, Muckie?"

The two snorted in laughter at their own attempt at humour.

82

"Who are youse? What do you want?" Duck snapped, his grip tightening on the hurley.

"Hey, man, de Duck talk English!" the redheaded boy said in mock surprise.

"Nearly!" his friend added. More snorts of laughter.

"Clear off!" Duck muttered.

"Hey man, that's not very friendly. We come in peace!" the redhead pleaded.

"Yeh. We heard about you from your girlfriend."

"My girlfriend?"

"Yeh. Emer. She real sweet on you, man. She say you're a big hero!"

Duck advanced towards them. He could feel the hair bristling on the back of his neck. "Look. I said clear off—and mind your own business!"

"OK. Cool it, man. We're just being friendly. Miss Dunne gave us special leave to come over here. Didn't she, Burkey?" The redhead winked at his pal.

"Sure thing, Biffo."

"We heard you were a real good hurler, man!" The redhead suddenly unleashed a vicious puck of the hurling ball he carried in his hand. Duck had to swerve his head out of the path of the ball as he swung his hurley upwards to block it.

"Hey that's very good, man!" Biffo was genuinely surprised. "Now can I have my ball back?"

"Sure," Duck snapped, bouncing the ball a few times before driving it low and hard with all the strength he could muster. It cracked off Biffo's shin. The redhead howled with pain and danced around on one leg.

Duck quickly snapped up his own ball and drove it at the other boy. Burkey was totally off guard as the ball rapped his knuckles. Duck sprang towards the two wincing friends and picked up his own ball. "Now, clear off—before I call my friends from the jungle, man!" He shook the hurley threateningly at Biffo.

The two looked at each other before deciding to retreat, one hobbling along, the other squeezing his swollen knuckles into his armpit. Scutch snapped at their heels. Biffo turned around, his large face red with rage. "We'll get you for this, Blackie," he snarled. Duck shrugged his shoulders and turned back to the vegetable garden. On the way he drove the ball with a burning rage against the water-barrel. He flung the hurley after the ball and resumed weeding the carrots.

Granny Flynn had watched Duck's confrontation with the two boys from the cottage window. When the boys left, she thought of going out to console Duck but then hesitated and turned back to the fireplace. She poked the fire to life under a pot of potatoes. The sparks danced crazily around the pot.

"Well, Miss Nan Fallon, I hope you're proud of yourself now." Bridie McKenna and her daughter, Mary Frances, stood directly in Nan's path in the churchyard.

"Canon McDonagh was right. The devil is among us." Mary Frances smirked as she nodded in agreement with her mother.

"When are you off to the Magdalen, Nan?" she asked. Nan looked at the ground.

"We'll pray for your black soul when we go to Knock next week. Come along, Mary Frances." Mother and daughter turned sharply and suddenly Nan Fallon was alone in the churchyard.

The sparks died away. Granny Flynn took a few sods of turf from the basket and propped them around the fire. The sound of a car crunching over the gravel track woke her abruptly from her reverie. Instinctively she tightened her grip on the poker and made her way to the door. A bright red car with zig-zag yellow striping pulled up sharply at the edge of the paddock. Pounding music echoed loudly from within the car. A tall lithe figure emerged carrying a small black object in his right hand. He smiled broadly. "Hi! Would this be Granny Flynn's place?"

"It would. And who—"

"And you're Granny Flynn?"

"I am—and who might you be?"

"Tony Tobin, from Westwave."

"Westwave?"

"Your local radio station. Westwave—making waves all over the west! I hear you had some excitement here last week."

"We had a couple of visitors," Granny Flynn replied cautiously.

"And what's this about a little black hero?" he asked, pulling a microphone from his pocket and fumbling as he connected it to the tape-recorder he carried in his right hand. Granny Flynn made no reply. "Could I have a few words with him—for my morning show?"

"No you could not!" Granny measured her words carefully and coldly.

"But it's a great story. Human interest. David and Goliath—"

"You'll take your machine and your fancy car now and you'll go—before I let the dogs out." Granny slapped the poker into her left hand.

"Look, Granny. I'm just doing my job. I'll treat this thing sensitively—"

"Tom," she called, without taking her eyes off the visitor. "'Tis time to let the dogs out."

"OK. OK. I'm gone!" Tony Tobin raised his hand in surrender as he backed away to the car.

Blind Tom came to the door as the car tore down the incline in a cloud of dust, the music inside pounding louder than ever. "Who was that?" he asked.

"Just some fellow trying to make waves," Granny Flynn replied with an impish giggle.

Chapter 11

The Visitor

E mer dreaded lunchtime at school. Class time was all right. At least she could busy herself with schoolwork and Miss Dunne could maintain a sort of order in the classroom. There had been uproar when she had sent for Biffo Power and James Burke, only to discover they were no longer in the corridor. They had left school altogether. Miss Dunne called to their homes that evening and when the two returned to school the next day, they protested that they thought she had sent them home. James Burke could not write. He had a badly swollen hand which he said was due to a fall.

Now in the playground Emer felt isolated. Nobody said anything directly to her but there was a lot of whispering and giggling in the background. Biffo in particular attracted a large group around him and there were hushed conversations, interrupted by laughter and occasional quacking sounds. When school was over, Emer was first out of the yard on her bicycle. For once Johnny's endless questions and Marion's complaints were a welcome distraction.

On the Wednesday afternoon her father brought Marion and Emer to the hospital. Emer was taken aback by her mother's appearance. Her head was sunk deep in the pillow and her face was as white as the pillow-cover.

She smiled weakly in welcome. Emer fought back the tears as she kissed her mother.

Marion dominated the conversation as usual. Emer sat at the end of the bed. It felt as if she were looking into a glass-walled room.

"...first exam is on Monday. English. Of course I'm studying—four hours a night. I wish people would understand the stress. Johnny's fine—but a nuisance. I mean how can I study and look after him? Emer? Emer has a busy life, haven't you, Emer? Oh—I almost forgot! I brought you some flowers from the garden," Marion said, stuffing the flowers into a vase next to the bed.

Her father interrupted Marion and the visit was over. Emer ached to stay with her mother but her father gestured towards the door. "Mam is tired now," he said quietly. On the way out, their father went with the ward-sister to meet the surgeon. The girls were left to wander out to the car. On an impulse Emer hung back and, when Marion went outside, she dashed back to the ward and her mother.

"What's troubling you, love? I could see you were unhappy, but Marion—here, sit beside me and tell me your news." She ran her fingers through Emer's hair as Emer told her in brief of her meeting with Duck and their adventures since that meeting. "And now Daddy won't allow me to see him and everyone at school is laughing at me!"

Her mother cupped Emer's hands in hers. Emer noticed how bony and white her mother's hands had become. "Your dad's only doing what he thinks is best for you. I'll have a chat with him. And as for everyone at school—if you're really sure about Duck, then stand by him. They'll come around. Would Duck not come down to the school?"

Emer was surprised by the question. She shook her head. "He's spent most of his life running away from schools and homes." She sat in silence, savouring the comfort of her mother's hands. For these few moments, everything was all right.

"Now give me a kiss. Your dad is waiting for you." The hands were withdrawn. She kissed her mother on the forehead. "Don't forget to give Johnny a hug for me," her mother said.

On the journey home, Emer broke the silence. "Will she be all right? What did the doctor say?"

"She's going to be OK—but she's not out of the wood yet. I hope you didn't upset her in any way."

Emer shook her head.

The week crawled by. School became a little more tolerable when Biffo Power was absent for two days.

"He has to help with the hay, Miss," his sister explained. In the playground Josie Byrne came up to Emer, proffering a bag of crisps. "Want one?" she mumbled. Emer was glad to take a crisp or two. She was even more glad of the company.

"God, I dread next week," Josie sighed.

"What's next week?"

"The sports. I hate it. All that running and stuff. And Mr O'Neill says everyone has to take part. Think I'll go sick. Want a bit of my sandwich?"

"No thanks," Emer laughed. "The sports won't be that bad, Josie."

"Indeed it will. Mr O'Neill made me go in the sack race last year. Only got a few yards and then I got stuck in the sack. Want a swig?" She held out a bottle of orange. Emer shook her head.

"Would you—would you go in the three-legged race with me, Emer?" Josie's eyes widened in appeal as she tilted the bottle upwards. Emer laughed inwardly at the thought of herself and Josie as three-legged partners, but Josie was being a friend—something Emer needed badly at that moment.

"Of course," she said.

Josie bounced up and down in delight, "You will? You're a star, Emer. Thanks! I hope we get farther than I did in the sack race."

On Sunday afternoon Tubberfinn's under-14 hurling team played its second match in the county championship. Their opponents were Kilconnell.

"If we don't win this handy, we may give up for good," her father said at breakfast. "Are you all coming?"

"Johnny and I will be there, won't we Johnny?" Emer said.

"Come on Tubber!" Johnny roared.

"That's it!" his father laughed. "We need lots of support."

"Well you can hardly expect me to be there," Marion announced. "I have my first exam in the morning and I have to reread my novel and go over my poems yet. And as for *Romeo and Juliet*... I'm going to fail, sure as eggs."

The match was tense. Tubberfinn was easily the better team but could not convert its superiority into scores. Kevin Healy paced up and down the sideline, urging on his team. Emer and Johnny shouted until they were hoarse, even though it hurt Emer to support Biffo Power. Tubberfinn held on to win by two points. Kevin Healy was not at all happy with his charges. "If you play like that against Castlerickard, the match will be over at half-time. If you forwards don't wake up next time, we'll have to find someone to replace you."

Duck was overcome with joy. He had brought a crust of bread to feed the swans. When he arrived at the little cove where he usually met them, there wasn't a sign of them initially. "Welcome to the club," he muttered. "Everyone seems to have forgotten me." He began idly to throw pieces of bread into the water. Just then the procession rounded the promontory that guarded the cove—the two swans, serene and watchful, followed in Indian file by five puffy grey cygnets. Duck chuckled at the contrast between the parents and the chicks. The swans, as always, glided through the water with effortless grace. The cygnets, however, were paddling furiously to keep in line.

"So that's your secret," Duck whispered. "Came to show them off, did you! They're beautiful. I'll have to bring a loaf of bread next time!"

The cygnets clambered onto a crude bed of broken reeds while the swans rode the wavelets that lapped the shore, occasionally pecking a piece of bread from the water but never straying from the busy cygnets. Duck lay flat on his belly, resting his head on his hands, engrossed by the scene. He wished Emer were with him to share it.

"My, but you've brightened up since you went out this morning!" Granny said when Duck eventually came back to the house. He told her his secret. "Well, I'm glad you have something to cheer you up. You've been moping a bit these past few days. I thought you were getting a bit restless...."

"Just haven't seen anyone."

"Meaning Emer?"

91

"Suppose so." He traced the toe of his shoe in a circle through the gravel.

"Why don't you go to see her?"

"In the school? You must be joking!"

"People know about you now. I'm sure that fellow on the radio has mentioned you."

"Are you trying to get rid of me?"

"No, love. You can stay here as long as you want. You know that. But you need friends—young friends. Now, go and dig me a bucket of spuds, like a good lad."

"History homework, children!" Miss Dunne chanted the words in expectation of great results. "We were to find out all we could about the First World War, weren't we?"

Emer groaned. She had forgotten all about it. The trick now was to look very interested and eager to answer—and hope you weren't asked!

"Well, James Burke, can you tell us when the First World War happened?" James looked totally mystified and shrugged his shoulders.

"Maybe your partner Liam Power can help us?"

Biffo gave a sheepish grin. "It definitely happened before the Second World War, Miss." There was an outburst of laughter and cheers.

"Children, please," Miss Dunne pleaded. "Jenny Gavin, tell us when the First World War started," she snapped.

Jenny was never to get an opportunity to answer the question. Paula Power's shriek startled everyone in the room. "It's him! The blackie!" All eyes followed her outstretched hand pointing to the window at the end of the room. There, with his face pressed sideways against the glass, was Duck, his hand held up to shield his eyes from the strong sunlight.

"Emer, is this your friend?" Miss Dunne called amid the growing din.

"Yes, Miss."

"Well, go and see what he wants!"

Emer beckoned Duck away from the staring eyes of the classroom. He followed her into the porch. "What on earth are you doing here?" she asked.

"Didn't I tell you? I'm going straight. I'm an inspector of schools now!"

Emer smiled in embarrassment. He was always too sharp-witted for her.

"I came to see you," he added quickly, deepening her embarrassment, "seeing as how you weren't coming to see me."

"I couldn't—I wasn't allowed—I had to—"

"Look. Stay cool, will you. Just tell me what happened."

Emer sighed. This wasn't going to be easy. "Everyone—at school, at home—was praising me for preventing the robbery. I had to tell them who the real hero was."

"What did you do, shout it from the roof of the bleedin' school? It's no wonder there were radio reporters looking for me!"

"Really?"

"Well one, anyway. So why couldn't you tell me this before now?"

This was the hard bit. "My dad wouldn't let me."

"Why?"

"He just thought...."

"I was a bad boy. The black fellow. The wog. Don't worry. I'm used to that."

"He'll change. If he met you—"

"Well he won't!"

"He's in charge of the under-14 hurling team. You could get a place...."

Duck laughed heartily.

"You could—if you tried."

Miss Dunne put her head around the corner. "Emer, are you not going to invite your friend in?"

"No – I'm going," Duck answered quickly.

Emer was surprised at her teacher's invitation. "No. Come in, even for a little while. They won't eat you," Emer suggested.

"I wouldn't bet. Two of them had a go already."

"Who?"

"One of them is a big redheaded fellow. I think he's called 'Biffo'."

"So that's where they went!"

"What?"

"Nothing."

"We're waiting, Emer!" Miss Dunne called.

"Coming!" She turned to Duck. "Please! It will make things easier for me."

He gave her a puzzled look, then shrugged his shoulders. "OK. But I'm warning you—if anyone starts trouble, I'll belt him!"

The reaction was instant when Duck entered the classroom with Emer. It was as if someone had switched everyone off. The hubbub became a frozen silence.

"This is Duck," Emer said nervously. A muffled "Quack" came from the back of the room. A few titters followed. "He's staying with Granny Flynn for a while." She stole a look at Duck, who was shuffling anxiously from one foot to the other.

"Take a seat, Duck," Miss Dunne urged. "It will be lunchtime soon—you can stay till then!"

To Emer's surprise, he slid into a seat nearest the door.

"Now, children, as you can see, Duck is just the same as yourselves except for one thing—"

Oh no, Emer thought. She's going to make a lesson out of it....

"He hasn't got a brain," Biffo sniggered.

Duck shot out of the desk, his eyes blazing. "You're the one who hasn't got a brain in that big head of yours saying things like that!" He pointed threateningly at Biffo.

Miss Dunne opened her mouth to intervene but instead the intervention came from an unexpected source.

"I know how Duck feels. You don't have to be black to feel like he does." The voice was low, halting at first, then growing in confidence. "Nobody bothers with me just because I'm fat. Well, nearly nobody." Josie Byrne smiled across at Emer. There was an awkward pause. "Emer is going to be my partner in the three-legged race in the sports."

"Who is going to be Duck's partner?" asked Miss Dunne. "That is, if he'd like to participate." Another pause. A few muffled comments. Miss Dunne was about to speak again but once more she was interrupted.

"Me," piped up Jenny Gavin.

Somebody shouted "Hurray!" and a burst of applause erupted in the classroom. Miss Dunne's effort to restore order only added to the confusion until the lunchtime bell signalled the release of the boisterous children into the school playground.

The children broke up into small groups as they ate their lunches and chatted noisily. Duck wanted to slip away but a number of curious children gathered around him. Biffo and his pals sat against the playground wall, still sniggering as they watched the group around Duck grow in size. An occasional "quack" could be heard above the laughter.

"I hope you can run very fast, Jenny," Emer said. "This fellow can fly."

"Well he can bring me with him when he flies," Jenny laughed.

"When is the sports anyway?" Duck asked.

"Friday," Jenny said. "You'd better be here."

"You'll all be wasting your time," Josie Byrne spluttered through a mouthful of food. "Nobody will stand a chance with Emer and me." She held out a crisp bag. "Want a crisp, Duck?"

Chapter 12

Sports Day

"**G**od, I hate maths!" Marion sighed. "Who invented them anyway? I mean, what use are they to anyone?" As usual she addressed her complaints to the world, but nobody was listening. Emer was reading Johnny a bedtime story.

"I mean 'sets' are the stupidest things anyone could imagine. A intersection B. What does that mean? I have two maths exams tomorrow and I haven't a clue. Does anyone care?" She flung the maths book away in exasperation. "Caroline O'Grady! That's what I'll do. Go down to O'Grady's and see if she'll give me a grind in this stuff. Little swot! Can't stand her at the best of times but this is an emergency. Emer," she called, "I'm going down to the phone-box to ring Caroline O'Grady and see if I can persuade—"

"Jiminy! I forgot," Emer cried.

"Forgot what?"

"I met Shane Joyce in Rigney's shop—"

"You what?" her sister roared.

"And he asked me to tell you to give him a ring."

"He WHAT?" Marion's incredulity had gone off the scale.

"Sorry!" Emer murmured.

"Sorry? You're given the most important message of

my life, something that's crucial to my whole future, and you FORGET it? And all you can say is 'Sorry'!" She mimicked a baby voice. "You little twot!" She grabbed her purse and made for the door.

"When Dad comes back, I've gone down to Caroline O'Grady's. Do you think you can remember that, twot? Caroline O'Grady—to study maths!" She slammed the door behind her.

"Why is Marion so cross?" Johnny asked.

"Why do giraffes have long necks?" Emer tweaked her brother's nose. "Because that's the way they're made! At least that's the way Marion is made as far as I'm concerned," she added absentmindedly.

"When are we going to see the jaffs, Emer?"

Oh no! Why did I mention them, she thought. "We'll have to wait until mammy is better, won't we? Now what about this little train in the story?"

"We could go in the train to see the jaffs, couldn't we?" Johnny asked sleepily.

Her father arrived home an hour later. "Where's Marion?" he enquired.

"I think she went to Caroline O'Grady's to study maths," Emer said quickly. The "I think" covers me, she thought.

"And Johnny?"

"Fast asleep."

"Good girl!" Kevin Healy's face wore a broad smile, something Emer hadn't seen for some time. He filled the kettle from the tap. "I have two bits of good news for you." His voice was noticeably lighter too. "Mum is much better. The doctor is very pleased with her progress and she'll be home in about a week."

"That's brilliant!" Emer was filled with delight.

98

Her father was rummaging in a kitchen press. "Marion Healy can never put anything back in its proper place. Where's my mug?"

Emer found it in another press. "And the other good news?" she asked, a little nervously.

"Oh, yes. Your mam spoke to me about this Duck fellow. Where did he get a name like that? You shouldn't have bothered your mam when she wasn't well, Emer."

Emer swallowed hard. He did say it was good news.

"Anyway," her father continued. "It seems I may have misjudged him a bit. Then who did I meet coming out of the hospital but your teacher. She told me about your man turning up at school. It's just as well I bump into these people. My own family never tell me anything!"

"I was going—"

"Anyway, Miss Dunne was impressed by Mr Duck and by the way you stood up for him. I suppose nobody is as black as he's painted!" Emer gave her father a playful frown. "Well, you know what I mean," he said. "But for heaven's sake will you answer me two things? Where did he get the name 'Duck' and what's he doing at Granny Flynn's?"

"That's a long story Dad, but one of the things he's doing is learning to play hurling."

"From Granny Flynn?" her father laughed.

"No, from Blind Tom."

"The blind leading the blind! Still, old Tom was a mighty hurler in his day. They say it was a disgrace he was never picked for the county team."

"Will you give Duck a chance on the under-14s?" Emer asked impatiently.

"Are you serious? What will they all say—a black fellow on the Tubberfinn team?"

99

Emer was annoyed with her father. "It doesn't matter what they say if he's good enough!"

"All right. Calm down! Calm down!" her father said, clearly taken aback. "Is he any good?" Before Emer could answer, he added, "We have a practice on Saturday morning. Tell him to come down and we'll see what he's made of."

Emer threw her arms around her father's neck. "Thanks, Dad! Can I go and see him now to tell him?"

"At this hour of the night? Certainly not! You can go tomorrow evening—if you make me a nice sandwich for my tea!"

"I'll make you the biggest, best sandwich you ever had!" Emer laughed.

Her father seated himself at the table by the kitchen window and opened out his newspaper. "You know," he called to Emer, "I could swear that was Caroline O'Grady that went by on a bike just now."

Duck had just lost another crack at the draughts title to Blind Tom. "You nearly had me there," the old man said with relief as he put the draughts back in the biscuit tin. "You lost concentration for a while. You have to keep the concentration up to the final whistle!" He began to fill his pipe from an old tobacco pouch. The reason for Duck's loss of concentration arrived at the door. Emer propped her bike against the wall of the house.

"You just lost me the draughts title," Duck said, opening the half-door. "I was watching you coming up the hill and lost my concentration on the game. Who could that stranger be? I kept saying to myself...."

"If you want, I'll go now," Emer said, reaching for her bicycle again.

"Oooh! Touchy, aren't we?" They looked briefly at each other. "Come on! No more messing!" Duck said with a winning smile. "I've got something to show you!" He raced up the hill through the Witches' Wood. Emer chased after him. When she eventually caught up with him just short of the lakeshore, he motioned to her to approach the water's edge silently. She padded behind him, puzzled at his behaviour until they peered over a rock to observe the swans patrolling a reed bed not twenty metres from where they were standing. Emer was about to ask a question when Duck put a finger to his lips and said quietly, "Wait." Moments later the parade of cygnets appeared from the reeds. Emer was totally captivated by them and nodded her approval to Duck.

Suddenly Duck groaned, "Oh no! Only four! They've lost one!" One of the swans became distressed, flapping its great wings and uttering a peculiar cry. Then to the relief of watchers and watched, a fifth cygnet scurried out of the reeds, obviously very frightened.

"Reminds me of Josie Byrne, always being late," Emer laughed. "Oh! I've got a surprise for you too. Dad says you are to come down to the under-14s' practice on Saturday morning!" Duck's reaction disappointed her. He continued to watch the cygnets intently.

"Well?"

"Well what?"

"You could say Great! Or Brill! Or even thanks! I did ask him for you!"

"Thanks."

"Don't fall over yourself thanking people."

"I'll write you a ten-page letter, all right?"

Emer bit her lip and turned to go. Duck finally turned away from the swans. "Look, I appreciate what you did.

101

It's just that I don't think it's a good idea."

"Why?"

"It's too much hassle and aggro. Can't you imagine Biffo and his pals; how they'll react if I turn up?"

"You're well able for them."

"I know. I'm afraid I might kill one of them if he tries anything on."

"That's not an answer. And anyway, you have more friends than you think. You should hear them at school. They're all asking when you'll come to school again."

"Ha ha! They'll be lucky!"

"You can't run for ever, Duck."

"I never said I was staying here forever."

"No. But for as long as you are here, you can be one of us. Play hurling for us. And look what you did for Josie Byrne. Everyone is amazed at what she said, especially Miss Dunne."

"OK. I'll see—but I'm not promising anything."

"You'd better not let me down. I told Dad you were brilliant!"

The field next to the school swarmed with children on sports day. A running track had been crudely marked out with whitewash. Mr O'Neill marched up and down, occasionally barking into a megaphone and looking very important with a clipboard which he consulted every few moments and on which he noted all the results. The races for the little ones were held first, so that they would not have to wait around. A warm sun beat down on the participants. Emer scanned the field anxiously for Duck and was disappointed to find no trace of him. Josie Byrne arrived in a brilliant red tracksuit.

"There's no way we can lose, Emer," she said. "I feel

it in my bones and I've been dieting all week."

"Dieting?"

"Mmm! Haven't eaten a crisp since Sunday."

Mr O'Neill called for competitors in the three-legged race. "That's us!" Josie cried. "Come on, Emer!"

Jenny Gavin came along. "Where's Duck?" she asked anxiously.

"I don't—There he is!" Emer cried pointing to a familiar figure crouched over the bars of Granny Flynn's bike, which skidded to a halt at the entrance to the field. He wore a baseball cap back to front.

"Come on Duck," Jenny called. "What kept you? Were you in the slow bicycle race?"

"Very funny," the breathless Duck replied. "I had to avoid the village. I'm still on the hop, you know. I kind of got lost for a while."

"You got lost in Tubberfinn?" Jenny laughed.

"Well, all them little roads are the same, aren't they?"

Mr O'Neill gave a final call for the three-legged race.

"Come on. That's us!" Jenny grabbed Duck by the arm and they dashed down to the start where they tied their legs together.

"On your marks!" It was the look on Josie Byrne's face that was Jenny's undoing.

"Get set!" She had her eyes fixed on the finishing tape and as she waited she bit her lip constantly. Emer was dwarfed by her partner, who clutched her tightly as they bent down awaiting the off.

"Go!" Josie suddenly came alive, screaming as the two of them lumbered up the track. Emer hung on to Josie's tracksuit and tried to match her steps. Jenny couldn't help giggling at the sight and sound of the pair ahead of her. The giggles became helpless laughter and she and

Duck had only run twenty metres when they collapsed in a heap on the track. The finishing tape was rushing towards the remaining runners. Josie was now screaming hysterically at Emer, half-dragging her partner as they stumbled to the finish and dived across the line.

"First place to the McCarthy twins!" Mr O'Neill barked into the megaphone. "Second—Josie Byrne and Emer Healy."

"Ah sugarlumps!" Josie panted.

"Never mind, Josie," Emer whispered, gulping air as she extricated herself from under Josie's body, "we'll still get a prize."

"Not enough! I just wanted to be the first at something for once in my life."

Jenny and Duck limped in last. Jenny could only point at Josie and start giggling again. "Next time I'm going with you," Duck said to Emer with some annoyance. "All this one can do is laugh!" All four disentangled themselves and lay back to recover from their efforts.

Josie sat up quickly. "As of now my diet is over. I'm going down to Rigney's for an ice-cream cone." The other three smiled and relaxed under the warm sun. A voice spoke from behind them.

"You didn't do much in the three-legged race, Quack!" It was Biffo. "Why don't you try a real race like the hundred metres? Or maybe you're going in the girls' hundred metres?" James Burke was sniggering behind Biffo. Duck clenched his fists.

"Aah, would you ever take a running jump at yourself, Biffo?" Jenny Gavin snapped.

"I'll be in the hundred metres all right," Duck said. "And you'd better watch out 'cos if I'm behind you, I'll eat your legs!"

"I suppose that's what they do in the jungle all right," Biffo laughed. Duck jumped up but the two troublemakers were swaggering off through the crowd.

"Don't mind him," Emer said. "Biffo is all talk and nothing else."

"Duck! Duck!" the muffled and excited voice of Josie startled the trio. She was in a very distressed state, breathless and with a mouth smeared with ice-cream which she had obviously tried to eat while running. She flopped down beside the others, fighting to regain her breath. "You—have—have—to—hide!" She forced each word out.

"Hide? Why? What's wrong?"

"Met a—man—down—at—Rigney's," Josie panted. "He was—asking—about you."

"What was he like?"

"Very—tall. Crew cut. Big—pointy—nose!"

There was a frightened look in Duck's eyes. "It's Foley! 'The Beak' Foley, from St Mark's!" As he spoke, a small black car with tinted windows cruised slowly past the entrance gate, turned in the school lay-by, came back and stopped at the gate.

"That's him," Josie squealed. "That's his car!"

Chapter 13

"The Beak"

The car door opened and a very tall man emerged, sunglasses perched on a huge hooked nose. He was dressed in a dark suit and stood for a moment flicking something from one of his sleeves.

"That's 'the Beak' all right," Duck whispered as he slid behind the three girls. For once he was glad of Josie's ample girth. The three girls froze momentarily, wondering what 'the Beak' was going to do next. Emer was quickest to react after the initial shock. On the nearby hedge she noticed a sack which had been discarded after the sack race. She scampered over to the hedge, keeping her eye on the stranger all the time, grabbed the sack and scurried back.

"Quick, Duck, Get into that!" She threw the sack at him. "All the way in—and lie flat. We'll use you as a pillow." Duck needed no second telling. He did as Emer bade him in a moment.

"If he goes down to Mr O'Neill, we're in trouble," Jenny whispered.

"Easy on, Josie," came the muffled voice from within the sack. "You're bleedin' smothering me!"

"Sorry!" Josie mumbled. The other two suppressed a giggle.

The stranger took a few steps towards the gate, all the

time scanning the entire field.

"Go away, Beak. Go away!" Josie whispered almost as a prayer. As if in answer, the stranger turned quickly back to his car, got in hurriedly, and sped away.

"Well done, Josie," Emer laughed. "Your spell worked!"

"'Twasn't my spell. It was what I told him down the village."

"Which was—"

"That Duck was around here all right, but he found the place boring and took off a week ago for Limerick!"

"Good on you, Josie!" Jenny slapped her on the back.

"Can I come out now?" Duck pleaded.

"Of course. Your friend 'the Beak' is well gone!" Jenny said.

Duck struggled out of the sack. "If that was being your pillow, I'd hate to be your mattress!" he spluttered.

"Tell us about 'the Beak'," Emer said.

"He's a pain," Duck replied. "Fancies himself as a sort of private investigator. He works for St Mark's, but he's always poking his big nose in where it doesn't belong."

"I hope it belongs in Limerick," Josie sighed.

"If it doesn't, he'll be back!" Duck said.

The megaphone voice of Mr O'Neill interrupted their thoughts. "Boys hundred metres. First, Liam Power. Second, Dara Malone."

"Damn!" Duck said in disgust. "Biffo will think I chickened out!"

The sports concluded early when a thunderstorm brought torrential rain sweeping across Tubberfinn. Duck and Emer sheltered in the school bicycle shed until the rain had eased into a fine drizzle.

"Are you coming back to Granny's?" Duck asked.

Emer looked at her watch. Ten to one. She didn't have

to be home until four. "All right! You haven't had a reading lesson for a while."

Duck blinked in surprise. "You're worse than Frosty-face!" he said.

They told Granny about 'the Beak' turning up in Tubberfinn. "You'll have to be careful for a while," Granny said. She looked out through the half-door into the thickening mist.

"They came in looking for me too," she said. "To Dunrickard House. Mrs Lyons was very good to me. She lied to them. Told them no one of my description was around the place. I never left the house for six months. Mrs Lyons, God be good to her, kept me going with books. I'm sure the library people wondered how she got through so many books...."

"Which reminds me," Emer said. "It's reading time!"

"Well it's a day for reading, anyway," Granny mused. "Have you something to read?"

Emer looked at Duck. "Yeh, well I'm only learning. I never learned at school, so Emer is teaching me." He scuffed his foot nervously on the stone floor.

"Why didn't you tell me that before now, child?" Granny put her hands on Duck's shoulders. He shrugged them gently. "I could help you too!"

The children went up to Duck's bedroom. "This is really cool," Emer said. "I wish I had a room like this." Her eyes fell on the photograph by the bedside. "Is that your—"

"Yeh!"

"She's lovely. And that's you! You're so tiny."

"Babies usually are."

"But you're *tiny* tiny."

"Yeh. Come on. Let's get the school bit over."

"You still miss her?"

"Sort of. She's my ma, isn't she?"

Duck approached the hurling field apprehensively. There were about twenty boys scattered around the field wearing an assortment of jerseys, tracksuits and helmets. Their voices echoed across the field as they called for a hurling ball to be hit towards them. In their midst he could pick out all too easily the distinctive red head of Biffo. He sighed and thought of turning about and going back to the Island, but just then Kevin Healy arrived in his car. Duck was relieved to see Emer and Johnny in the back.

"Dad, this is Duck," Emer announced.

"How are you, Duck?" Kevin Healy offered his hand. "I hear you're nifty with the *camán*!"

"Don't know...."

"Well, we'll find out soon enough." He blew a whistle to call the boys together.

"Hi Duck!" Johnny came running towards him, hurling a rubber ball. "Are you going to play with me?"

"Hi Johnny!" Duck flicked the ball away and lifted it onto his hurley. "I have to play with these fellows first." He allowed Johnny to knock the ball away.

"Good luck!" Emer called.

"Thanks."

Kevin Healy stood in the middle of the group. "This is Duck," he said. "Most of you know him already. He's getting a trial for a place on the team. That might make some of you sit up." There were a few splutters of laughter. "We have a match against Castlerickard on Tuesday. They had a big win in the first round, so it won't be easy. We'll have a bit of backs and forwards now.

109

I want to see some tight marking and some good scores."
He divided the group into sets of backs and forwards and
threw in the ball.

Emer was horrified to see that her father had put Duck
at full-forward to be marked by Biffo Power! She tried to
catch his attention but her father was far too involved in
the action, urging and criticising, to notice her, and she
knew he would be annoyed if she intervened directly.

"They should have called you 'Chicken', not 'Duck'.
You funked the hundred metres," Biffo taunted him.

"I was tied up at the time," Duck snapped.

"The first ball that comes in here—you'll be tied up
again!"

Duck moved away but Biffo shadowed him wherever
he went. At last the ball came towards them, low. Duck
sprinted forward and bent down to catch it. He had barely
grabbed it when Biffo's hurley caught him across the
knuckles. The searing pain was matched by Duck's anger.
He swore at Biffo as he swung his hurley at Biffo's shins.
Kevin Healy jumped in between them whistling
furiously. "We'll have none of that," he shouted.

"He tried to take my hand off!" Duck complained,
holding up a hand that was a mass of weals.

"Dangerous play, Biffo. Free in!" Kevin Healy wagged
a threatening finger.

"It was a fifty-fifty ball," Biffo pleaded.

"Free in," Kevin Healy repeated. "And as for you," the
finger turned to Duck. "Keep your temper under control.
There's no place for hotheads on this team." Duck
glowered at Biffo. "There's obviously no love lost
between you two, so I'm separating you," the trainer
continued. "Dara Malone, you swap places with Duck."

The game continued without further incident. Duck

was mostly ineffective, though he did manage to score a point. His hand throbbed with pain, especially when he gripped the hurley. He was glad when the practice game ended. Kevin Healy called them together for an assessment of the game before they disbanded. "Don't forget. Be in good time on Tuesday night," he reminded them. "Everyone here at 7:30. That includes you, Duck."

Emer came over to Duck. "I saw what Biffo did. He's an animal!"

"Can we play now, Duck?" Johnny asked.

"Just a little game, I've only got one hand!"

"Disgraceful!" Granny spat the word out as she bathed Duck's swollen hand. "To do a thing like that deliberately." Duck sucked his breath in sharply as Granny touched a tender spot.

"You'll get many a skelp in your hurling career," Tom said from his chair in the corner. "But hitting back never pays. You've got to beat him by craft—be faster to the ball or cleverer with it!"

"That's all right if you haven't lost an arm or a leg in the first minute," Duck said, grimacing with pain.

"That's true," Tom laughed. "But at least young Power will be on the same team as you next time out." He reached for the biscuit tin on the shelf above him. "Anyway, you still have one good hand for playing draughts! Do you fancy a crack at the title?"

"Well honestly, Tom Flynn," his wife said. "Do you ever give the poor child a rest?"

"'Tis good training for the hurling," Tom chided her. "You have to watch your man, anticipate his move, get in fast for a score."

"It's OK, Granny," Duck said as she bandaged his

knuckles gently. "It feels better already. You'd make a good nurse!"

"I've had practice galore with himself," she said. "And before! And before...."

Mary Walsh had terrible trouble with sleep-walking. She slept in the bed beside Nan in the dormitory. Nan was a light sleeper and usually the creaking springs of Mary's bed woke her as Mary began her walk. If the springs didn't wake her, Mary's crying would. Mary always cried when she walked in her sleep. She sobbed and sniffed as she called gently, "Mo leanbhín! Mo leanbhín! Cá bhfuil mo leanbhín?" (My baby! my baby! Where's my baby?) searching between and under the beds.

Nan had learned how to deal with sleep-walking—pour some water from the wash-jug on the floor in front of Mary and when she stepped on the water it woke her up gently. Nan would then bring Mary back to her own bed.

One night for some reason, probably an extremely hard day in the laundry, Nan didn't wake up in time. Mary Walsh wandered all around the dormitory in search of her baby. She then prised open the big window with the frosted glass. Everyone wondered afterwards how she had managed it since it had always been stuck fast. Mary then attempted to clamber out through the window when the heavy frame came crashing down on the knuckles of both hands. Her screams of agony and shock echoed through the building, terrifying the rest of its inhabitants. Nan sat up with Mary Walsh that night, and for many nights afterwards, bathing and bandaging her raw and swollen knuckles....

Chapter 14

Preparations

"Brunelleschi...Buonarroti...Renaissance...." Marion slammed her history book shut. "Why do all those guys have names you can't either spell or remember? God! Another glorious failure tomorrow! I mean, why can't they have names like Axl Rose or Bono or...."

"Shane Joyce?" Emer couldn't resist the temptation.

Marion turned on her. "Listen, Miss Smartypants. Be very careful with your comments. Actually, if you really want to know, Shane Joyce and I could be an item very soon—if I can persuade him to ditch Tracy Forde."

"Shouldn't be hard," Emer said. "After the way herself and Tommy Dolan were carrying on at mass this morning!"

"At mass? With Tommy Dolan? Tell me more!" Marion discarded her history book.

"There isn't any more. They were just giggling and chatting all through mass."

"God! Have they no shame or respect? Wait till Shane hears that!" Marion's eyes lit up. "Thanks, Emer. You're not a bad kid. Not a bad kid at all!" She sauntered out of the room. "I think I'll take a break from my studies," she called back over her shoulder. "I need to take a walk."

"To the telephone kiosk, I suppose," Emer muttered.

A large crowd turned up on Tuesday night for the match against Castlerickard. Kevin Healy assembled the Tubberfinn players and read out the team. There was no place for Duck, but he was included among the substitutes. "This is it, boys," the manager said. "Win this one and you're in the final. Go out there and support each other. And keep the marking tight. These lads are good!"

His words proved true: Castlerickard got away to a furious start and were four points ahead before Tubberfinn settled down. Encouraged by the home crowd, they gradually drew level and went ahead just before half-time.

As the second half began, the chants started. "Come on Tubber!" and "Tubb-er, Tubb-er" echoed around the field. A long clearance from Biffo Power fell to Dara Malone, who whipped the ball into the Castlerickard net. The crowd went wild. Duck felt a hand on his shoulder. "All right, Duck, here's your chance to prove yourself," Kevin Healy said. "Go in there at right-half forward in place of Jimmy Kelly."

Duck took some time to get over the surprise. He was on a team. His first time. A buzz went through the crowd. He knew they would be asking questions. He had to do well—not for himself, but for them—for Kevin Healy and for Emer. For Granny and Tom. His opponent got an even bigger surprise. "Where did you come from?" he asked in genuine amazement.

"Never mind where I came from. It's where I'm going that counts," Duck replied, setting off towards the goal. He found he had the speed to beat his opponent—if only

114

he could get the ball. Since the ball seldom came down his wing, he found he had to go in search of it. Soon he heard Kevin Healy roaring at him. "Duck! Will you stop wandering all over the field and stay in your place!"

Duck shrugged his shoulders and did as he was told. Eventually the ball did come his way and he scored two points. "That's it, Duck! Now we're hurling!" Kevin Healy shouted. Suddenly it was over. Tubberfinn had won by five points, but Duck was only starting to enjoy himself. He wished the match could have gone on. Instead, he was being slapped on the back by people he had never seen before. He felt a light smack from a hurley on his bottom. He looked around and found Biffo winking at him. Instinctively, he winked back.

"You still have a lot to learn, Duck," Kevin Healy said. "There are fourteen other fellows on the team. Each of them has a job to do. You can't run around the whole field trying to do everyone else's work. You wouldn't last ten minutes that way. But you're learning!" He gave Duck a playful jab and then addressed the entire team.

"OK, lads. Again, well done. The big day is Sunday week. The final against Lackabawn. They've demolished every team they've met so far, but they're not unbeatable. I want the whole parish to turn out for that match. Athenry, Sunday week, three o'clock. But first we'll have a practice on Saturday."

"Don't mind Dad," Emer said as they cycled home. "He really thought you were great. So did I."

"Thanks. But he was right—about running around the pitch. I'm not used to working with others. It's something I have to learn."

"If you came down to the school it would help," Emer suggested.

"Oh yeh?"

"Yeh! Think about it."

They parted at Brennan's Bridge.

"Think about it!" Emer shouted back, her voice echoing in the still summer evening.

Granny and Tom were childlike in their excitement over Tubberfinn's victory. "And you scored two points! Sound man, Duck!" Tom said, sucking his pipe furiously. "Imagine! Tubberfinn in a county final again! Begor, I'll be in Athenry for that!"

"Tom Flynn, will you have sense?" Granny chided him gently.

"Try stopping me! We've waited over forty years for this." He reached for the biscuit tin. "Now, Duck. How about another crack at the title?"

Thursday was the happiest day Emer had experienced for a long time. It was one of those rare days when everything fell into place. When she arrived at school she found to her delight that Laura Daly had returned to school and was seated at the table they shared.

"I had to come and see this boyfriend of yours that everyone is talking about," she said, "and that my best friend never even mentioned," she added pointedly.

"He's not my boyfriend. He's just my friend. And I couldn't tell you about him because it was a secret then."

"It's certainly no secret now!" Laura laughed. "When am I going to see him?"

Laura's question was answered at lunchtime when Duck appeared in the school-yard. He immediately became the centre of attention. Biffo and his pals remained in the background and made no attempt to taunt Duck.

"He's cute," Laura said. "No wonder you kept him a secret!"

"Very funny!" Emer replied. She was tiring of all this teasing.

When the bell rang for class, Miss Dunne approached Duck and invited him to stay. He was reluctant to do so, mindful of his last visit, but the teacher persisted and Duck took his place at the front of the classroom. As soon as Miss Dunne had set the class a geography project, she brought several books down to Duck and sat beside him, speaking in a hushed tone and occasionally calling out loudly to someone at the back to behave. She spent a long time with Duck. Emer watched them nervously. She hoped Duck would not discover that she had had a word with the teacher about him. This time she hadn't kept a secret....

On Thursday evening came the best surprise of all. Ann Healy came home from hospital. She was still very weak and would be confined to bed for some time yet, but she was home. The emptiness was filled. The house at once seemed brighter and warmer. Johnny burst into tears, climbed on to the bed for a cuddle and would leave only when his mother promised that she would still be there in the morning. Even Marion, once she had voiced her complaint about the Business Studies paper that morning, was overcome with happiness and lay beside her mother for a long time, sniffling quietly.

On Saturday after hurling practice, Emer invited Duck back to her house to meet her mother. Duck was unusually quiet and shy and spoke only a few words.

"She's nice," he said eventually as they rode back to the Island.

"You'll like her even more when she's better, stronger." Their bicycles bumped along the causeway. "What about your own mum?"

"What about her?"

"Do you ever think about going to see her?"

"Yeh, but...." His voice trailed away. "I'm going to see the swans," he announced suddenly.

They ran through Witches' Wood, playfully tossing pine-cones to each other. When they reached the cove, the swans were very restive. Duck sensed a hostility that wasn't there before. When the cygnets appeared, he could see why. They had grown considerably and their feathers had lightened in colour. But there were only four of them.

"Look!" Emer pointed to the reed-bed where they had last seen the cygnets. There were feathers strewn around a tiny crumpled and half-eaten carcase.

"Josie Byrne!" There was a rage within Duck as he swung a kick viciously at a pine-cone. Emer remembered how they had laughed at the cygnet when they had last seen it waddling out of the reeds behind the others. "She was a loser," Duck said, his voice trembling. He drew another kick at nothing at all. "She was a bleedin' loser, that's all."

As the week before the under-14 County Final dragged by, excitement grew in Tubberfinn. Green and white flags began appearing in windows. The window of Kelly's supermarket was decorated entirely in green and white. Even Mrs Rigney covered the faded corn flakes boxes in her shop window with a large poster trimmed in green and white. Above a pair of crossed hurleys, the words COME ON TUBBER stood out in bold green lettering.

Duck spent most of the week building a rick of turf in the haggard. A trailer-load of turf had been delivered on the Monday and Duck had followed Tom's guidance and example in building up a rick that would protect the turf from winter rains. Duck marvelled at the dexterity of the blind man as he laid out the foundation of the rick, bent on both knees. The two of them slowly built up the rick, using the sods of turf like building blocks. There was great satisfaction in seeing the rick take shape and, as it neared completion, Duck had to work from the top of a ladder. Granny brought tea and scones and the two sat back against the rick and savoured the food. They talked about the upcoming match and the great interest the entire parish was taking in it.

"It's very important for a little place like Tubberfinn," Tom said. "We don't get much to shout about, so this is our chance! And it's very important for you young lads. If you win on Sunday, it will give you the heart to keep at the game. Mind you, it will take some winning. Those Lackabawn fellows have a great tradition. In my day, they were the devil to beat. Tough as teak, so you'll need to be sharp!" He grabbed a rung of the ladder to haul himself to his feet. "Now there's a thing I forgot entirely! Go in there, Máirtín, and get the hurley and *sliotar*!"

Duck, slightly puzzled, did as he was told.

"Now," Tom said, straightening the ladder against the turf-rick, "take about twenty paces back from here. What you have to do is take a shot and drive the *sliotar* under the bottom rung. Then between the first and second rungs, then between the second and third and so on."

"Aw, come on," Duck protested.

"The only thing is, if you miss any one of them, you

119

have to start at the bottom again!"

"You must be joking!"

"Go on, give it a try. It will sharpen up your shooting no end. Myself and the 'Thresher' Larkin used to have great fun doing this!"

Duck shook his head and took a shot, just to please the old man. It was well wide of the mark.

"Come on now. Concentrate!" Tom said, his voice taking on a more serious tone. Duck gritted his teeth and tried again—and again. He finally found the range. "Up the ladder with you now," Tom said. "And no cheating."

Duck gave a loud whoop as the very next shot sailed between the first and second rungs. However, the next shot missed the ladder altogether and Duck had to start all over again. He was hooked on the game now and over the next couple of hours it became an obsession with him.

Tom wandered back into the house but he could tell Duck's progress from the whoops of delight alternating with howls of frustration. "'Tis a heartscald all right," Tom chuckled. "I remember it myself!"

In the end Granny had to go out as dusk was falling and plead with Duck to come in.

"How did you do?" Tom enquired.

"Only four," Duck said with disgust.

"That's good, that's good!"

"Not good enough. I'm going all the way up tomorrow, if it kills me!"

On the Saturday morning the team assembled for a light puck-around and a pep-talk from Kevin Healy. When Duck got back to the Island, he headed straight for the turf-rick, but Granny summoned him to the kitchen. She handed him a large carrier bag. "This is for you, from

Tom and myself!" she said proudly.

Duck opened the bag slowly. Inside was a complete hurling kit—helmet, jersey and togs, socks and boots. "Kevin Healy helped us," Granny said. Duck shook his head. He couldn't find words to say. Instead he gave Granny a hug.

"There's only one thing missing," Tom said, producing a hurley from behind his back. It wasn't a new hurley and had obviously been scrubbed clean. Duck looked over the fireplace. Only the outline of Tom's hurley remained in the soot and dust on the chimney-breast. "I know what you're thinking," Tom said. "'Tis nearly fifty years old, but there's the best of ash in it. 'Tis a bit big for you, but you'll manage it. And seeing as how it helped Tubberfinn win a county title before, it might do so again!"

"T-thanks," Duck muttered. He swung the hurley and twirled it in his hand. It was much heavier than Marion's hurley, but he could cope.

"Out you go now," Tom said, "and see how far up the ladder you'll get with that stick!"

That evening the biscuit tin was taken down as always. Tom played his usual cautious game, taking long sucks on his pipe as if for inspiration. Duck studied every move intently until Tom moved a king, which left him exposed on one side. Duck moved in to take a king and a man. The match was over.

"Well, fair play to you!" Tom said. "You've won the title at last!"

"You let me win," Duck said as he gathered up the draughts.

"No, I did not!" Tom was very firm. "Don't think that for one minute. I lost my concentration—the very thing

I warned you about. Let that be a lesson to you!"

"Yeh," Duck laughed. "That really was a silly move you made. What were you dreaming about?"

"I was thinking too much about tomorrow's match— and the last time we won. God, Máirtín, ye just *have* to win tomorrow!"

Chapter 15

The Final

A fine drizzle gave way to hazy sunshine on Sunday morning. There was only one topic of conversation in Tubberfinn. Old men leaned against the churchyard railings and discussed the under-14 team's success.

"'Twill be a greasy sod...."

"They'll have to be sharp. They say the Lackabawn fellows are jumping out of their skins."

"A few early scores would settle them...."

Father Regan concluded mass with a prayer for a fine day and victory for Tubberfinn. "The important thing is that we enjoy our day out. It's not often that Tubberfinn gets its place in the sun. This is our day and we'll make the most of it. Our young men will do us proud. I have no doubt about that. A win would be nice but we will accept the Lord's will." He paused for a few moments. "But if we lose by a last-minute point, we'll be back here next Sunday wanting to know why. Come on Tubber!" he roared, his voice echoing through the church as first giggles and then applause greeted his words. That set the mood for the day.

Four of Tobin's buses were quickly filled with happy, noisy supporters. Ireland soccer jerseys and scarves were adopted as Tubberfinn colours. In Malone's Bar and Lounge the atmosphere was enlivened by Tom Kelly's singing of "The Men of '49", a ballad recalling Tubberfinn's last major victory.

Duck was nervous. He had spent some time shooting at the ladder but could not get past the first rung. His failure only increased his anxiety. Granny prepared a light lunch but he found himself unable to eat. The morning crawled by. The minibus would collect him at Brennan's Bridge at one-thirty. It was time to go. Granny and Tom wished him good luck.

"We'll be there shouting for you," Granny said. "The Gavins are giving us a lift later on."

Tom put his hand on Duck's shoulder. "Just keep your head," he said.

Duck made his way along the causeway, beheading thistles with his hurley. The whole thing seemed like a dream. If anyone had told him a month ago that he would be living in redneck country—he smiled as he thought how much that word would annoy Emer—and on his way to play in a county hurling final. Hurling! A game he had only seen once at a distance from his dormitory window in St Mark's.... St Marks. It seemed a thousand miles away and yet he could still smell the cabbage from the kitchen, could still see the mustard walls of the dormitory, could still hear Groucho's whining voice echoing down the corridor.

He reached Brennan's Bridge and walked a short distance down the road before seating himself on his hold-all on the grass verge. A car came over the bridge. It was the Gavins on their way to collect Granny and Tom. "Good luck, Duck," Jenny roared out the window. He waved to her. "Come on Tubber!" Jenny's voice trailed away.

It became very quiet again. Suddenly there was a

great whirring noise overhead. It was the swans, their necks stretched like gun barrels, feet tucked in, great wings moving in unison. Duck waved nervously to them. Were they leaving in anger? In sorrow? Maybe they were wishing him luck....

He never heard the car purring over the bridge. Its surprised driver couldn't believe his luck as he eased the car to a halt within a few feet of the boy. Duck was startled by the hand that fell heavily on his shoulder. "Well, Martin, isn't this a great stroke of luck!" Duck froze as he recognised the nasal tones of "the Beak" Foley.

Before he could move, the hand clamped his wrist. "A great stroke of luck indeed! I've put up a lot of mileage tracking you down, Martin, but your little holiday is over now. Come on!" He dragged the boy towards the car.

Duck resisted violently, attempting to swing the hurley across "the Beak's" shins, but the man's strength was too much for him. He wrenched the hurley from Duck's hand and shoved the boy roughly into the car through the driver's door. He tossed the hold-all in after Duck and thought of flinging the hurley away, but then wedged it alongside his own seat and slid in behind the wheel. He switched on the ignition, flicked a switch and turned to Duck with a leer. "Internal locking system. Keeps us all nice and cosy!" The car sped off down the narrow road.

"I have to play in a hurling match—the county final," Duck protested.

"Yes, Martin, I am intrigued by this. You of all people, hurling! You see, I've kept track of your progress. Amazing what you can pick up on local radio and in the papers. Do you know what one paper said about you? 'The nippy little winger, Martin Duck, notched two useful points for

Tubberfinn!' So I came down to see this 'nippy little winger' and here he is waiting obligingly on the side of the road for me! Well I'm afraid, Martin, that your request for a transfer has been turned down. You're still a St Mark's player!" He gave a hollow laugh and pressed hard on the accelerator.

Kevin Healy marched over to his daughter who was standing propping a huge teddy-bear dressed in green and white up on the boundary wall of the pitch. "Where's Duck?" he asked.

"I don't know," Emer replied. "He was to come on the team bus."

"Well he didn't, and it's twenty to three. If he doesn't turn up in the next five minutes, he's off the team."

"The Beak" Foley was humming along to a classical music tape. "Do you not like Bach, Martin?" he enquired. "Very relaxing music." Duck was far too desperate to relax. They had travelled fifteen, maybe twenty miles along what seemed a circuitous route. He looked at the clock on the dashboard. Ten to two. He would have to do something. He looked around the car. Nothing out of place. Spotlessly tidy. Typical "Beak".

As if reading the boy's mind, "the Beak" leaned across to brush some dandelion seeds from the dashboard. As he did so, a tractor came around the corner at some speed. Its youthful driver swung desperately into the ditch to avoid the oncoming car. This manoeuvre only caused the buck rake which was attached to the tractor to swing in the opposite direction. There was a crunching, grating sound as the outer arm of the rake tore along the side of the car, scoring deep into the bodywork and shattering the windows on the driver's side.

"The Beak" gave a shriek of pain as the car lurched violently before becoming embedded in the hedge. Duck was thrown forward, banging his head off the sunshade above the windscreen. After the terrifying noise came an unreal silence. Duck was temporarily stunned. He shook his head in an effort to dispel the ringing sensation within. He glanced across at "the Beak", who was slumped across the steering-wheel uttering low moans.

It took Duck a short while to realise that his opportunity had come. He leaned across and flicked the door-locking switch. He grabbed his hold-all and opened the rear door, crawled across the back seat and after much manoeuvring, dislodged the hurley. He clambered out on to a grassy bank, leaped over the low hedge, and took off across a recently cut meadow. He heard the dazed tractor driver calling on him to come back but he kept running—anywhere, but away, far away from "the Beak".

Emer stood on the embankment scanning the approach road to the hurling ground for any sign of Duck. What could have happened to him? Granny and Tom had arrived and confirmed that Duck had left the house to catch the team bus. And now he had disappeared.... Suddenly she caught a glimpse of a familiar figure weaving his way through the spectators. She shouted his name and waved furiously. He acknowledged her wave and made for the turnstile. Emer dashed back to the dressing-room to inform her father.

"But I am, I'm telling you, I am playing for Tubberfinn," Duck pleaded.

"Oh yeah—and I play for Aston Villa!" the turnstile operator laughed.

"It's all right, Tom. He's one of ours." The voice of Kevin Healy came from the other side of the turnstile.

"Begor, I've seen everything now," the operator sighed as he allowed Duck through.

"What in God's name kept you?" Kevin Healy asked, glancing anxiously at his watch.

"It's a long story. I'll tell you later," the breathless Duck replied.

"You have one minute to get togged out. Go!" The trainer barked, pointing to the dressing-room.

"What happened to your head?" Emer called after him.

"Bumped into a 'Beak'!" came the reply.

The noise reached an almost frightening level as the match began. One of the Lackabawn supporters led the chants for his team on a *bodhrán*. Not to be outdone, the Tubberfinn supporters resorted to a rhythmic hand-clap which built up to a resounding shout—TUBBER! Duck felt a throbbing in his head from the accident. The last thing he needed was this din.

Lackabawn were a big team, and very strong, as Duck discovered in his first clash with his opponent. They also settled much more quickly and scored three points without delay. Then came disaster. Biffo, at full-back, completely misjudged a high ball and the Lackabawn full-forward swept the ball to the net. Six points down and little more than ten minutes gone. Biffo gradually made up for his error with some good interceptions and long clearances. Tubberfinn were gaining more possession but the scores were not coming. Duck eventually broke free from his marker and scored a point. He was almost sure he could hear Blind Tom shout,

"Come on the Island!" He instinctively patted the hurley. Later he won a free which Dara Malone pointed. The half-hour flew by and Duck could scarcely believe it when the referee blew the half-time whistle. Lackabawn—a goal and seven points, Tubberfinn—four points.

"Them fellows are more than fourteen. Look at the size of them!" panted a breathless James Burke.

"And the hairy legs!" someone else added.

"Don't mind the size of them," Kevin Healy rasped, as he paced up and down. "You are the problem, not them!" The team looked at him with some puzzlement. "This is a team game. You're all forgetting that. You're all running around playing your own little games. All trying to be heroes. Shooting from impossible angles. Wandering out of position. You should be supporting one another. Covering off. Looking up for a better-placed colleague." He spoke in short bursts, staring at all of them. "Now get out there and play like a team, like a Tubberfinn team!"

His words brought an immediate change to the Tubberfinn team. Their play was tighter, more organised. Gradually they whittled away Lackabawn's lead. Duck scored another two points. He forgot about his headache. The tension among the supporters was unbearable as the gap between the teams narrowed. Three points. Two points. Kevin Healy moved Biffo to centre-field in a desperate effort to get Tubberfinn ahead. Amid all the noise Duck kept hearing Tom's quiet voice. *Keep your head! Keep your head!* Dara Malone pointed another free. One goal and ten points to twelve points. There could only be minutes left.

Tubberfinn launched another attack. There was a resounding clash as two opposing hurleys drew on the ball which spun high into the air and directly into

Duck's path. The Lackabawn defence charged after the ball. It seemed to hang in mid-air as Duck weighed his options. He could hear the Tubberfinn fans roaring. "Blast it over the bar! Bury it!"

The angle was tight. *Keep your head.* Then his eye picked out a distinctive red head which had slipped in behind the defence. *Keep your head.* Lob it into the rainbarrel. A hand went up beside the red head. The ball was coming down. *Keep your head.* Duck swung the ancient hurley upwards. He weighted the stroke perfectly over the charging defence into Biffo's path. Biffo caught the ball cleanly and slammed it to the net.

The Tubberfinn roar was deafening. Biffo turned, wild-eyed and red-faced, and charged straight at Duck. His expression suddenly turned to delight and he raised his hand to exchange "fives" with Duck before racing back to the centre of the field. The last couple of minutes were a blur to Duck. The play swung up and down the field. Screams of anguish came from both groups of supporters. And then a beautiful, long shrill blast from the referee's whistle. It was over. They had won. Tubberfinn had finally won the under-14 championship!

Duck and his colleagues barely had time to embrace each other before they were engulfed in a tidal wave of green and white, led by Kevin Healy, who danced his way around the whole team, hugging each one of them individually. The supporters descended on them next, slapping them on the back, hugging them, lifting them in the air. Flags were held proudly aloft and the "Tubber" chant grew in volume as the delirious fans savoured victory.

Emer suddenly appeared from the throng and threw her arms around Duck's neck. She then whispered in his ear. He nodded and began fighting his way through the crowd towards the terrace. He was playfully thumped and shoved but eventually reached the wall where Granny and Blind Tom stood. They were both in tears. Duck punched the air in delight. "We did it!" he cried.

Granny bit her lip as she reached out to cradle Duck's head. "'Tis the proudest day of our lives," she whispered, her voice spent with emotion. Tom nodded and reached out to pat Duck's head. "Good man, Máirtín. You kept your head and you did it!"

A sort of order was eventually restored to enable the cup to be presented to Dara Malone. The cheers echoed across the pitch. No one, neither the players nor supporters, wanted to leave the field. Father Regan ran around like a crazy man, cigarette in mouth, shaking every hand he could. Tubberfinn had won its place in the sun.

Chapter 16

Celebrations

Bonfires blazed in greeting as the team bus approached Tubberfinn. Small roadside fires at first and then a huge fire outside the hurling pitch. Flags hung from windows. Green and white teddies sat on gateposts. The entire parish seemed to have squeezed into the car-park outside Malone's Bar. The team had been brought for a celebration meal in Athenry before setting out on the victorious return home. Duck lay back on his seat and closed his eyes. It had been quite a day. He wondered what had happened to "the Beak". He hadn't been too badly injured as far as Duck could ascertain, but his car was a mess. That would hurt "the Beak" even more than his own injuries. He would be out of action for a while but he would be back. Duck would have to make a decision soon.

The bus inched its way through the clamouring throng towards an open-backed lorry that would serve as the welcoming platform. There was a tumultuous roar as the team eventually fought its way out of the bus and onto the lorry. Somebody started the TUBB-ER chant and the entire crowd took it up, clapping as they chanted. Father Regan jumped up on the platform and conducted the chant for a while before appealing for calm. He addressed the crowd.

"We've had a great day, the biggest day in Tubberfinn

for many a year, and we owe it all to these young men, of whom we are rightly and fiercely proud." A mighty cheer went up. "They haven't just won a championship. They have united a parish, a whole community, something that is very important in these times. So for that we thank them." Another roar. "And we must thank the club officials for all the work they have put into the team and all the other teams over the years." A burst of applause. "We must especially thank one man for his dedication to this team of heroes, and that is their trainer, Kevin Healy." He gestured to Kevin to come forward as the cheers erupted once again. Kevin shuffled to the front and waved to the crowd which began chanting "Speech! Speech!" Emer was bursting with pride as she cheered her father.

"I'm not one for speeches," Kevin began, "but I just want to say how proud I am of this bunch of lads. They're the best—we knew that all along, but now the whole county knows it!" A huge roar went up. "I'd just like to introduce each one of them to you." As he did so, each player stepped forward and waved to the crowd, some shyly, others relishing the public acclaim. Kevin left Duck until last. "What can I say about this fellow? I don't even know his proper name. We know him as Duck!"

The chant went up—Duck! Duck! Duck! Duck! He waved embarrassedly to the crowd.

"The amazing thing about this young man," Kevin continued, "is that he never hurled until a month ago. And you saw what he did today! That pass to Biffo was pure hurling—hurling with the head." There was another burst of applause.

"I'm afraid I can't take any credit for training him. That goes to that man over there—Tom Flynn, probably the greatest hurler Tubberfinn ever had." He pointed to the hunched figure perched on Malone's window-sill. A new chant went up—Tom Flynn! Tom Flynn! Tom Flynn! Tom dismissed the acclaim with a wave of his hand but the mention of his name was a cue for Tom Kelly to leap up on the lorry and sing, yet again, "The Men of '49". The players were eventually allowed down from the lorry to mingle with the crowd.

"It's like when Ireland came back from the World Cup," Duck said to Kevin as they pressed through the crowd.

"For Tubberfinn, it is the World Cup," Kevin replied. "We even have the video. They're going to show it inside now."

For now, Duck needed space. He made his way out to the fringe of the crowd, where Emer was waiting for him.

"I have to go home now—to be with Mam," she said.

"I'll go with you," Duck said.

"But the celebrations—you'll miss all the fun."

"I've had enough for one day," Duck sighed.

"Yes, what did happen—with 'the Beak'?" Emer asked.

Duck was interrupted by a breathless Josie Byrne, who came running up to them clutching two bottles of orange in one hand and two packets of crisps in the other. "Where are you going?" she panted. "Malone's are giving free orange and crisps to everyone under 14. Isn't that brill?"

"I have to go home," Emer laughed.

"You can have our share, Josie," Duck added.

"No," Josie pressed the orange and crisps into Emer's hands. "Take these, I can get more. Bye!" She was already on her way back to Malone's. "And Duck," she called.

"Yeh?"

"You played deadly in the match!"

134

"Thanks."

"And I think you're cute!" She was gone.

"Always knew she fancied you," Emer teased. "Now tell me what happened!"

Duck told her how "the Beak" had abducted him, of the accident and his subsequent escape.

"But how did you get to the match?"

"Hitched. I can read signposts now, you know!" He flashed her a broad smile.

"What about 'the Beak'? He knows where you are now."

"That's the problem. He'll be back, so I'll have to make myself scarce."

"What will you do?"

"I don't know. I haven't had time to think about it yet."

"Well done Duck, you were brilliant!" Marion greeted them with unaccustomed cheerfulness. "Tell me, little sister, is beloved father in good humour?" She tweaked Emer's nose playfully.

"Of course he is—and you certainly are!"

"Why wouldn't I be? We won the match, the Junior Cert is over—never mind if I failed half the subjects and—wait for it—Shane Joyce has asked me to Blazes Disco to celebrate! As long as Father approves.... Life is beautiful, sister!" She preened herself in front of a mirror. "Rather like myself, don't you think?"

Tubberfinn's victory had been a tonic for everyone, no one more so than Emer's mother. She gave Duck a big hug, much to his surprise, and quizzed the two on every aspect of the game. "And what about Dad?" she asked.

"Dad's the big hero. He even made a speech!" Emer laughed.

"A speech? He's certainly on a high! What's happening now?"

"Half the parish is squashed into Malone's watching a video of the match."

"I know what we'll do." Her mother's eyes danced as they hadn't done for a long time. "We'll get hold of the video and we'll have our own little party to celebrate! How does that sound, Duck?"

"Yeh, cool," Duck said, looking out the window.

Emer felt embarrassed for her mother. "Duck is a bit worried about something, Mam, I'll tell you later."

"I'm sorry," Duck said after an awkward silence. "I'd better get back to Granny's."

When he got back to the Island, Granny and Tom still had not returned. He propped a chair against the fireplace and replaced Tom's hurley on the chimney-breast, securing it by the nails that had been driven into the wall forty years previously. He found an envelope and pen and wrote a message.

Gone to bed, Duck. Up Tubber!

He stood the message on the kitchen table and went up to his room. It had been a long and eventful day.

Tubberfinn recovered very slowly from the celebrations the following day. The children had a day off school and most families took the opportunity to sleep in. Duck spent much of the day in the garden. It was a strange day, matched by an oppressive humidity. That evening Emer was playing hurling in the garden with

Johnny when her mother screamed her name from the living-room. She froze momentarily before dropping the hurley and racing into the house, terrified of what she might find. Her mother sat rigid in the chair pointing to the television. The gaunt drained face of an ill woman looked out from the screen. Emer stood transfixed as the voice of a news-reader spoke.

"Ms Kelly, who is suffering from AIDS, made an impassioned plea to her son, Martin, affectionately known as 'Duck', to come home." A photograph of a younger Duck replaced the gaunt figure.

The voice continued: "Martin—or Duck—is thought to be somewhere in the West of Ireland. He is twelve years old and of stocky build." The gaunt figure came back on a split screen next to a photograph of her son. She spoke hoarsely and very slowly. "Come home, Duck, son. I need to see you. Come home, please—"

Emer felt the tears welling in her eyes as she looked frantically at her mother, who smiled weakly through her own tears. "Go—now," she whispered. "I'll be all right. Go!"

Chapter 17

The Return

Emer tore across the causeway on her bicycle. Her eyes kept misting over. Her mind was a blur of images she had seen on the television screen. She pedalled furiously up the incline, jumped from her bike, letting it roll aimlessly onwards as she dashed in the door. Granny and Tom sat on either side of the fire. Granny kept shaking her head, her tear-stained face glistening in the firelight. "He saw it here," she sobbed. "He's gone. He just ran up to his room and then out the door. I don't know where—"

Emer turned and raced to the door. Twice she almost fell, first when she tripped over the yelping Scutch and then when she stumbled over her own bike. She staggered up through Witches' Wood, her side aching with a stitch. She careered downhill again, through the clearing and on to the cove.

Duck stood at the water's edge. He threw a stone viciously at the water and turned to her. "Don't say anything!" he roared. "Anything! Anything! Anything!" He kicked at the little waves that lapped the shore. Emer sat on a rock, gripping her side and fighting to regain her breath.

"They're gone too!" He gestured towards the empty cove. "Gone! Everything's gone. Everything's—finished! Everything!" He collapsed into a sitting position and took something from his shirt pocket. It was the photograph. He cradled it in his hands, and stared at it. "That wasn't my mum on the telly. It wasn't!" he shouted. "Was it?" he turned to Emer. She nodded.

"Wasn't. She was grey—and old—and ugly." He buried his head in his hands, thumping it against the framed photograph. He began to sob loudly. Emer sat there, unsure of what to do. It hurt her to see him in pain like this, but she was afraid to do or say anything lest it might upset him more. She sat there for a long time, letting him talk and cry. When he had exhausted himself, she said quietly. "Let's go back to the house."

To her surprise, he stood up and turned to go, clutching the photograph tightly in one hand. She followed a short distance behind. When they emerged from the wood, he stopped abruptly. There was a car parked outside Granny's house.

"It's all right," Emer said. "It's our car."

"I don't want to see anyone," Duck muttered.

"You don't have to. Daddy probably just came for me. He won't say anything."

What neither of them expected was that Emer's mother was there also. Ann Healy walked slowly towards Duck, took him in her arms and held him there for a long time. An occasional stifled sob came from Duck. Each time it did, Emer's mother gently caressed his head. Eventually she could not remain standing any longer. Her husband guided her to a chair but she held on to Duck's free hand and gently persuaded him to loosen his grip on the photograph in the other hand.

"She's beautiful," she whispered. "You must go to her, Duck. You know that. She's very ill."

Duck nodded.

"Good boy," whispered Granny Flynn. "Good boy."

"Can Emer come with me?" Duck's voice was barely audible. "Not to my mum, just to Dublin."

"Of course," Ann Healy said. "We'll arrange it. And you know, Duck, you can always come back here. We'll arrange that too. Now, I think we all need a good night's sleep."

Kevin Healy came to collect Duck on the Wednesday morning. Tom took Duck's hands in his. "God go with you, *a Mháirtín, a mhic.* We'll miss you and that's for sure. You'll have to come back to give me a crack at the title!" Duck nodded weakly.

Granny took him in her arms and spoke softly to herself....

"Come on now Nan," Sister Agnes said quietly. "It's time."

"Just let me hold him another while, Sister. Another little while." She clutched the tiny bundle lightly to her body and began to sing quietly to the infant.

"The longer you hold him the harder it is," Sister Agnes said.

"I just want him to be asleep," Nan whispered, taking up the song again. The infant drifted into sleep. Nan smiled down at him. "You'll come back to me, a stóirín."

Sister Agnes eased the bundle out of Nan's arms and quickly slipped out through the door and down the long corridor.

"You'll come back to me, *a stóirín,*" she lilted softly as Duck kissed her on the forehead and eased himself from her arms. He took up his hold-all, patted Scutch on the head, forced a hoarse "Goodbye" from his dry throat and hurried to the waiting car. As the car rumbled over the causeway he glanced back. Blind Tom waved from the doorway. There was no sign of Granny Flynn.

Emer accompanied Duck on the Wednesday bus. Marion and Johnny went also—Marion to help out and Johnny to see the giraffes in the Zoo. The bus journey was uneventful, except for Johnny's incessant questions which tested Marion's patience. Emer and Duck sat together in silence. When they reached Dublin, Duck went with them on a bus to the Phoenix Park. "It's not too far from here," he said. "You know how to get back?" Emer nodded.

"Where are the jaffs, Emer?" Johnny asked.

"Just round the corner," Emer said.

Marion and Johnny said goodbye to Duck and moved away.

"Well, good luck," Emer said with a sigh.

"Thanks for everything," Duck said. "You're not bad—for a bunch of rednecks," he laughed.

Emer punched him playfully, then kissed him on the cheek. "G'bye," she whispered. She turned and ran after Marion and Johnny.

That evening they settled themselves on the Galway bus. Johnny was overcome with excitement and exhaustion and collapsed into sleep before the bus left Dublin. Emer had not stopped thinking of Duck all afternoon. Had he met his mother? How had it gone? Would he stay with her? Would he ever come back to Tubberfinn?

Marion gave a huge sigh. "God, it's going to be a boring summer. Bo—ring! Just my luck! Shane Joyce is working with his uncle in Limerick! It's just not fair."

Emer closed her eyes and stretched out her legs. Her feet came in contact with a bundle under the seat in front of her. No, she thought. No, I'm not even going to open my eyes....

Also by Poolbeg

When Stars Stop Spinning

By

Jane Mitchell

Tony is fifteen and doesn't want to go back to school. Despite showing terrific talent on the clarinet, he'd rather get a job with his brother on a building-site.

When a joyriding accident lands Tony in *Lismore*, a Dublin rehabilitation centre where he is sent to recover from severe head injuries, he meets Stephen, also fifteen, a gifted musician and composer who has a wasting disease.

This is their story and that of their friends who, together, refuse to let their difficulties stop them from confronting life's challenges head-on.

When Stars Stop Spinning is a brilliantly told story of friendship, courage and ultimate success and introduces a striking new talent in Jane Mitchell.

Also by Poolbeg

The Hiring Fair

By

Elizabeth O'Hara

It is 1890 and Parnell is the uncrowned king of Ireland. But thirteen-year-old Sally Gallagher, "Scatterbrain Sally" as her mother and young sister Katie call her, has no interest in politics. She is happy to read books and leave the running of the house to those who like housework.

A shocking tragedy changes the lives of the sisters. Instead of being the daughters of a comfortable Donegal farmer and fisherman, they have to become hired servants, bound for six months to masters they don't know.

Elizabeth O'Hara has written an exciting story that has its share of sorrow and joy. She creates in Scatterbrain Sally a new and unforgettable Irish heroine.

Also by Poolbeg

World Myths & Tales

By

Carolyn Swift

This is a collection of twelve mythological tales, from places as far afield as India, China, Japan, Australia, New Zealand, Canada, North, South and Central America, Persia, Egypt and Black Africa. Appropriately, in this "Year of Indigenous Peoples", there are myths of the Maoris, the Aborigines, the Basutos, the Canarians and the North American Passamaquoddy tribe.

Dragons, giants and a variety of monsters figure in many of these tales, but there are also stories of evil and ambitious kings, independent-minded women and mischievious boys, as well as of remarkable animals and birds, from snakes and giant lizards to llamas and parrots. Several creation myths are included, which tell of the lighting up of the sun, the shaping of the world and of how people escaped the great flood.